AFTA SpringerBriefs in Family Therapy

A Publication of the American Family Therapy Academy

Founded in 1977, the **American Family Therapy Academy** is a non-profit organization of leading family therapy teachers, clinicians, program directors, policymakers, researchers, and social scientists dedicated to advancing systemic thinking and practices for families in their social context.

Vision

AFTA envisions a just world by transforming social contexts that promote health, safety, and well-being of all families and communities.

Mission

AFTA's mission is developing, researching, teaching, and disseminating progressive, just family therapy and family-centered practices and policies.

More information about this series at http://www.springer.com/series/11846

Laurie L. Charlés · Gameela Samarasinghe
Editors

Family Therapy in Global Humanitarian Contexts

Voices and Issues from the Field

Editors
Laurie L. Charlés
Our Lady of the Lake University
San Antonio, TX
USA

Gameela Samarasinghe
University of Colombo
Colombo
Sri Lanka

ISSN 2196-5528　　　　　　ISSN 2196-5536　(electronic)
AFTA SpringerBriefs in Family Therapy
ISBN 978-3-319-39269-1　　ISBN 978-3-319-39271-4　(eBook)
DOI 10.1007/978-3-319-39271-4

Library of Congress Control Number: 2016940804

© American Family Therapy Academy 2016
This work is subject to copyright. All rights are reserved by the Publisher, whether the whole or part of the material is concerned, specifically the rights of translation, reprinting, reuse of illustrations, recitation, broadcasting, reproduction on microfilms or in any other physical way, and transmission or information storage and retrieval, electronic adaptation, computer software, or by similar or dissimilar methodology now known or hereafter developed.
The use of general descriptive names, registered names, trademarks, service marks, etc. in this publication does not imply, even in the absence of a specific statement, that such names are exempt from the relevant protective laws and regulations and therefore free for general use.
The publisher, the authors and the editors are safe to assume that the advice and information in this book are believed to be true and accurate at the date of publication. Neither the publisher nor the authors or the editors give a warranty, express or implied, with respect to the material contained herein or for any errors or omissions that may have been made.

This Springer imprint is published by Springer Nature
The registered company is Springer International Publishing AG Switzerland

Series Foreword

The AFTA SpringerBriefs in Family Therapy is an official publication of the American Family Therapy Academy. Each volume focuses on the practice and policy implications of innovative systemic research and theory in family therapy and allied fields. Our goal is to make information about families and systemic practices in societal contexts widely accessible in a reader-friendly, conversational, and practical style. We have asked the authors to make their personal context, location, and experience visible in their writing. AFTA's core commitment to equality, social responsibility, and justice are represented in each volume.

Family Therapy In Global Humanitarian Contexts: Voices And Issues from the Field brings issues of social justice front and center as practitioners working in the midst of war, cultural revolution, or the aftermath of disasters illustrate what family therapy looks like across borders and contexts. The authors describe how they confront the moral and practical dilemmas when persons trained in high-income countries seek to help people in low-resource settings. How do "importers" of knowledge look at themselves and turn to and engage with local people and local knowledge in the service of mental health and psychosocial support? How may family therapy practice and training be modified to fit the setting and high level of needs? How does one creatively work "in vivo," across multiple languages, while being sensitive to issues of colonization and transliteration of concepts developed in Western space, often when working outside their home country and in situations that can be dangerous?

The authors in this volume are from diverse cultural and sociopolitical contexts across the globe. They represent different disciplines and different levels of training and areas of expertise. Their accounts of their work are poignant. Readers are brought into the way the authors think, often transported into the setting itself as though you are there. The collection is a treasure of practical recommendations for anyone seeking to work across borders in humanitarian and conflict-ridden global contexts. It documents and explores complex issues of voice and language in the telling of their stories. For those like me who do not typically work in these settings, the volume offers a powerful experience, not only in seeing how the authors apply family therapy in their unique situations, but also as a window onto ourselves, challenging us to think about who we are and what we do from larger, global perspective. I invite you to join in the journey.

Carmen Knudson-Martin, Series Editor
AFTA SpringerBriefs in Family Therapy
Lewis & Clark College
Portland, OR

Contents

Introduction to Family Therapy in Global Humanitarian Contexts: Voices and Issues from the Field 1
Laurie L. Charlés and Gameela Samarasinghe

Knowledge Fair Trade 13
Marcela Polanco

Humanitarianism, Colonization, and/or Collaboration? Working Together in Uganda and the United States 27
Teresa McDowell and Paschal Kabura

Collaborative Therapy with Women and Children Refugees in Houston: Moving Toward Rehabilitation in the United States After Enduring the Atrocities of War 39
Manjushree Palit and Susan B. Levin

Ofreciendo Terapia En El Idioma De Preferencia Del Cliente: El Modelo De Preparación Profesional Calificada En Dos Idiomas De Ollu 51
Joan L. Biever and Jeanette Santos

Family Therapy in Postwar Kosova: Reforming Cultural Values in New Family Dynamics 65
Mimoza Shahini, Adelina Ahmeti and Laurie L. Charlés

Time, Trauma, and Ambiguous Loss: Working with Families with Missing Members in Postconflict Cyprus 77
Kyle D. Killian

Engaging the Humanity in Front of You: Family Therapy Task Shifting in the Context of Armed Conflict 91
Laurie L. Charlés

Family Therapy in Libya: Navigating Uncharted Waters 103
Malak Ben Giaber

**"My Son Is Alive": Is Family Therapy Appropriate for Families
of the Disappeared in Sri Lanka?** 115
Gameela Samarasinghe

**Kaleidoscopic Shifts: The Development of New Understandings
as Therapists "Go and Find out"**............................ 125
Catalina Perdomo, Deborah Healy, Daisy Ceja, Kathryn Dunne
and Kotia Whitaker

Introduction to Family Therapy in Global Humanitarian Contexts: Voices and Issues from the Field

Laurie L. Charlés and Gameela Samarasinghe

This volume represents voices in family therapy—practitioners, trainees, and specialists in family and psychosocial health—in different parts of the globe, and from unique field perspectives. In this introductory chapter, we describe each contribution to the volume, focusing on its relevance to family therapy practice as a set of ideas, as well as its connection to the ideas about global mental health in humanitarian contexts. In this chapter, we situate each contribution within the discourse of family therapy, introduce who we are as coeditors, and discuss how we approached and worked with the authors. We also offer an analysis of how we view each chapter as an illustration of the unique complexities and challenges of family therapy programming in humanitarian settings, and also of the creativity involved—in designing and delivering such programs, both in the present and in the future.

Introduction

Mental health and psychosocial support (MHPSS) needs in communities are radically different from place to place; this is especially so in a humanitarian setting, when it is the family who is the buffer against the stress of atrocities (Walsh 2007). Addressing barriers to psychosocial well-being in the low-resource setting of a humanitarian context requires creativity, humility, and, in structural terms, multi-sectoral partnerships (Tol et al. 2011). It requires local people and the local, tacit knowledge they hold about their community, as their definitions of health and

---

L.L. Charlés (✉)
Our Lady of the Lake University, San Antonio, USA
e-mail: lcharles@ollusa.edu

G. Samarasinghe
University of Colombo, Colombo, Sri Lanka
e-mail: gameela2010@gmail.com

healing are critical for any meaningful outcome. Professionals working in the humanitarian space must keep in mind the contextual realities of the region in which they work, and immerse themselves in understanding both "micro- and macro-level factors" that affect these communities (Catani et al. 2008, p. 173).

In this book, we hope to illustrate how family therapists think about and work in the humanitarian space. We present a set of chapters by authors who illustrate the use and relevance of family therapy work from a variety of voices, some originating in real time in a humanitarian setting (Ben Giaber; Charlés), others during or after a humanitarian disaster such as war (Killian; Samarasinghe; Shahini, Ahmeti, and Charlés). The voices and issues we have chosen to present in this volume also are reflective, critically examining the moral hazards of exporting family therapy to places and communities without sensitivity to history, that is, the historical appreciation of centuries of atrocities (Polanco; McDowell and Kabura; Palit and Levin). Yet families do not exist in a vacuum; nor do the practitioners who so often want to help them. Here we also present emerging voices in family therapy. In the final chapter, Perdomo, Healy, Ceja, Dunne, and Whitaker discuss, from their unique view as clinicians in family therapy training, the conceptual preparation, hopes, and curiosities about their future selves, working in global humanitarian settings.

As far as we know, this is the first book that addresses the role of family therapy in global humanitarian contexts. While we sought out a wide diverse group of authors, we found that there are many countries not included, many things we did not have the space to discuss, and many questions raised after we completed the editing of the volume.

Collectively, we see the volume as a platform that can enlighten all of us engaged in family therapy and global mental health in humanitarian contexts. Each chapter brings a different set of issues to the table. As coeditors, we are also part of the whole. We start this chapter with the context and ideas that brought us to work together in 2010.

Who We Are

Laurie Several years ago, while I was a Fulbright Scholar in Colombo, Sri Lanka—where I met my coeditor Dr. Gameela Samarasinghe for the first time—I had the idea for a book on the use of family therapy ideas in humanitarian settings. I am a family therapist trained in the United States, who has found herself working several times over the past decade as a trainer of family therapy in low- and middle-income countries and fragile, conflict-affected states.

I had arrived in Colombo during a period of intense reflection and generative thinking about my work; in the previous year I had worked as a family therapist/consultant in Egypt, Burundi, and Democratic of Congo—all intellectually stimulating and challenging projects that had sent my family therapy mind spinning. Although I had already worked in several other countries before arriving in Sri Lanka, something about this place, this time, was different. A year after the end of their three-decade civil war, I found myself in the midst of a community of people living through their first year of peace. Sri Lanka, too, was spinning with ideas.

At my desk one weekend in Colombo, I proposed a book to a publishing house in the United Kingdom. My query was answered within 24 hours. Then, in a day or two, I was asked for a formal proposal, which I quickly wrote. Of course, I was not offered a contract. In hindsight, I can see that while I had a vision, I was not ready to put together such a book. But I was certain about this: It was a book I very much wanted to read. I suspected I was not the only one.

Gameela When Dr. Laurie Charlés asked me to coedit Family Therapy in Global Humanitarian Contexts: Voices and Issues from the Field, I was very honored; however, I was not very sure whether I would be the most suitable person for this task, as I am not a family therapist. I am a clinical psychologist by training, but shelved all my clinical training and experience obtained in Paris when I came to work in Sri Lanka more than 20 years ago, in the midst of the war. I felt that I did not know enough about Sri Lanka and the Sri Lankan people, not having ever lived in the country, to provide them with psychological support. I had to start from scratch, learning how Sri Lankan people and particularly people affected by the war talked about and gave meaning to their suffering. After many years, when I felt a little more comfortable working in a setting that was becoming gradually less intimidating, I decided to think about how best I could support these people in a way that would be meaningful and helpful to them.

Clinical psychology was certainly not the answer. People in Sri Lanka did not perceive their issues as psychological problems. They related their problems to not having food to feed their families, to not having schools to educate their children, or to having lost their property, or having no place to pray as these had been destroyed by bombs. They did not spontaneously seek help from psychologists or counselors as it meant that they would have to talk about issues that were not fundamental to them. These professionals would not be able to renovate their children's school that had been destroyed or give them loans to rebuild their house.

When reading through the articles for this issue, I asked myself how family therapy would be applicable in Sri Lanka. Certainly, family is very important in Sri Lanka. In fact, both the extended family and the community play a very important part in all decisions regarding the family, including children's upbringing, household chores, finances, and so forth. Therefore, family therapy could well be a therapy to consider importing to Sri Lanka. For now, however, family therapy as it is usually thought of (i.e., as a focus on the interactions among family members) may not be the most "practical" of interventions, given the dearth of local professionals (and the absence of family therapists) in the psychosocial field, and also given the way in which the majority of people in Sri Lanka think about their well-being, especially those living in postconflict areas. Value is given more to the impact of wider systems and social contexts on people's lives, and therefore to addressing collective-level needs before those of the family and the individual.

The issues described in the articles point to many of the challenges I had to face when starting work in Sri Lanka at the time of the war. I spoke no Tamil and struggled in Sinhala. I had never traveled to most of the locations where I eventually worked. I felt I knew nothing about the people I met. I asked myself how I could support them when they had found their own coping mechanisms.

I understood that I had to go to them and not expect them to come for therapy when this would mean depriving themselves of their daily wage, making arrangements for children to be taken care of during their absence, and traveling long distances where transport is not easily available. And if other family members had to come for family therapy and for many sessions, what consequences would this have for them and for the members of their family who remained at home? These are some questions that are common to the articles in this issue. Reading the articles has encouraged me to further consider ways of adapting family therapy to the context of postwar Sri Lanka, as family therapy has been found to be a very useful intervention in other humanitarian situations.

The Role of Family Therapy in Low-Resource Settings and with Humanitarian-Affected Populations

In recent years, a number of family therapists have called for a more sophisticated approach to international aspects of family therapy training (Platt 2012; McDowell et al. 2012; Platt and Laszloffy 2010), including broader global perspectives on family therapy practice in academic and training settings (Wieling and Mittal 2002), and use of community-focused, strengths-based practice for families affected by war and violence (Landau and Saul 2004; Walsh 2007).

At the same time, however, while family therapists in the global North have often focused on curricula designed to meet requirements for licensure and regulation (Rivett 2010), a robust body of work in other disciplines, such as public health, international development, and behavioral economics, has focused on the effective delivery of services in humanitarian settings, including public mental health and psychosocial support services. Although the extant literature often illustrates an inherent systemic sensibility and strengths-based intention, family therapy, as a professional voice, has little presence.

In this volume we wanted to highlight family therapy voices and issues relevant to the practice of family methods in humanitarian contexts. The chapters represented in this volume reflect the diversity of multiple states (countries), and thus illustrate for us the unique contexts of family therapy in different parts of the globe. Not every chapter discusses a "case" of "how to do family therapy" in a global humanitarian setting, however. Rather, sometimes the "case" to discover is us, who we are as professionals, and the challenges we discover along the way.

This matter is particularly relevant for U.S.-based family therapists, who may hold limited knowledge of humanitarian settings, the effect of ongoing or previous atrocities on family and community life, and how these complex matters are cross-culturally relevant to the skill set they need in order to work proficiently in contemporary practice. As an example of the application of cross-cultural skill sets to a humanitarian-affected population in Houston, Texas, Palit and Levin (this volume) describe how they constructed and implemented a support group for Ethiopian refugees resettled in their city.

In humanitarian settings, there are often challenges to a country's (and a community's and a family's) infrastructure, resulting in basic needs for water, sanitation, functioning institutions (such as in the education, health, and financial sectors), and networks and community resources. Practicing traditional family therapy in such settings is often not conducive to meeting needs on the ground. That is, traditional family therapy practice is displaced to the background as community social supports and basic needs become more salient. Family therapists must adapt accordingly. And they do. As these chapters illustrate, family therapy is an approach that can be molded to the context, unlike other therapy models, which are often more prescriptive.

Analysis of the Forthcoming Chapters: Knowledge Transfer and Trade

As we were editing chapters on Gameela's second-floor patio in Colombo, inspired by the fluorescent green parakeets whizzing across the sky at dusk, Sonny the dog's constant protective barking at passing cars and rickshaws, and our first reading of the initial draft of Marcela Polanco's chapter, we had an "A-ha!" moment. Dr. Polanco's chapter uses the phrase *fair trade* as part of its title, but in a sense, we realized, all of these chapters are a kind of trade. Theoretically, gains from international trade are supposed to benefit each party to the exchange (that is, each state), and also to be mutually beneficial for society as a whole (Kowalcyzk 2006).

In the parlance of international trade, and specifically knowledge transfer (which is in a sense the trade of knowledge and technical skills across borders), there is an inherent assumption that knowledge is a good that "belongs to the world." Yet like all other goods, knowledge is not equally distributed across the globe: its allocation is inefficient. Further, its distribution is highly specific to conditions on the ground. Whom is the knowledge transferred *from*, and whom *to*, exactly? What does that transfer look like in the field? What conditions inhibit or promote it?

Unsurprisingly, social instability is one of the major deterrents to trade (Kowalcyzk, personal communication 2011). In the midst of social instability, even the most beneficial exchange of goods and services—which is what trade is theoretically designed to be—will fail. In those circumstances, even the most efficient allocation of resources becomes irrelevant. Yet therein lies the rub: social instability is a constant factor in humanitarian settings.

Because international aid tends to flow from high-income countries to low- and middle-income countries or to fragile, conflict-affected states (FCS), the issues of knowledge transfer and its effect on the situation on the ground play out in different ways. Further, in knowledge transfer terms we could also ask, does the channel through which the MHPSS product is delivered matter? What type of infrastructure (such as the human resource capacity) is there? What is the state or organizational capacity to implement the resource or product? In Kosova this has a relevant effect on the ability of war veterans to get family therapy services (as Shahini, Ahmeti, and Charlés suggest). Similarly, McDowell and Kabura discuss unfair and unequal distribution of mental health services in some of the communities they worked in in Uganda. They learned from the mistakes of others and modified their own work to try to avoid such conditions.

Description of Each Chapter

The chapter, "Knowledge Fair Trade" by Marcela Polanco, is a critical essay on what it means to import knowledge and training from Western white culture to other cultures. In her case, the other is Colombia, and also, herself. A family therapist who practices from a narrative framework, Polanco's chapter raises the questions one rarely hears in the midst of a humanitarian context, and it is the reason we present it first. Her chapter raises the specter of history, and of what we as family therapists think of as "context." Her contextual focus spans the topics of international relations across decades and centuries, of how these relations inform the present day, and the implications of what it means to do work from a global perspective.

The chapter by Teresa McDowell and Paschal Kabura, "Humanitarianism, Colonization, and/or Collaboration? Working Together in Uganda and the United States," centers on the question of how to engage in counseling-based humanitarianism across contexts shaped by unjust global power dynamics without compromising equity, fairness, and justice. McDowell and Kabura draw from their work across Uganda and the United States to offer a set of guidelines for engaging in what they term "collaborative humanitarianism."

The authors describe their work thus: "While our work does not fall within the strict definition of humanitarianism, it crosses over into humanitarian action and is informed by humanitarian ideals. We continuously consider the ethics of humanitarianism and the power of colonizing processes as we collaborate, share field knowledge, and redistribute resources across the global North and global South." They ask the question, "How do we engage in truly collaborative humanitarianism?" The metatext in the question, about the form and content of our efforts in the field of family therapy when it intersects with global mental health, is one that illuminates every chapter, but, as a prism, in very different ways.

The chapter "Collaborative Therapy with Women and Children Refugees in Houston: Moving toward Rehabilitation in the United States after Enduring Atrocities of War," by Manjushree Palit and Sue Levin, discusses the use of collaborative therapy (Anderson and Goolishian 1988), in the form of a refugee support group, and how they developed and modified their approach as they learned the community's needs and areas of interest. They also discuss elegantly their own growth and surprise as practitioners, and offer practical suggestions for how to do group work with refugees.

The chapter by Joan Biever and Jeanette Santos, "Ofreciendo Terapia en el Idioma de Preferencia del Cliente: El Modelo de Preparación Profesional Calificada en Dos Idiomas de OLLU" (Providing therapy in the client's preferred language: the OLLU model for professional competence in two languages), describes how a university institution in the United States became the first to offer psychosocial support training in Spanish to practitioners who would be delivering psychosocial support services in that language. It is a unique and yet sensible idea to design such a program, yet there are few programs like this in the United States.

Ironically, this philosophy is clearly appreciated in global mental health, where MHPSS practitioners are expected to receive their training in the language in which they deliver services. For example, international work contexts often expect one to speak at least two U.N. languages. Yet in the United States training family therapists to work in more than one language is a rare practice: there are only a handful of such programs in the country. In their chapter, Biever and Santos illustrate for us how they felt ethically compelled to create such a program, now nearly 20 years old, and they offer comments from graduates of the program as to how the training has informed their practice. Domestically as well as internationally, the capacity to perform multilingual training is a matter of human resources.

In the chapter "Family Therapy in Postwar Kosova: Reforming Cultural Values in New Family Dynamics", Mimoza Shahini, Adelina Ahmeti, and Laurie L. Charlés highlight how family therapy ideas, training and clinical practice have been implemented in the context of a postconflict state. The chapter focuses particularly on how the war, which ended in 1999, has changed family dynamics in the Kosovar culture. Their chapter illuminates the discontinuity between conflict and postconflict life, when identity during war—both of individuals and of families—can transform dramatically after it is over. "Veterans returned to their families with a great sense of pride for what they had achieved, yet immediately faced social and political pressure over what had happened during the war. Many of them were stigmatized because of international pressure against war crimes—the same social treatment meted out to everyone."

This chapter is also a useful illustration of task shifting, a scaling-up strategy used in public mental health that involves training professionals from specializations (such as psychiatry) to provide family therapy services. Task shifting or task sharing is a way of offering comprehensive mental health care services (such as family therapy) when state budgets do not provide necessary infrastructure for capacity building, a very common occurrence in low- or middle-income countries.

In "Time, Trauma, and Ambiguous Loss: Working with Families with Missing Members in Postconflict Cyprus," Kyle Killian discusses the effects of war on community and family life in Cyprus, and what he calls "a crucial dimension of trauma—the disruption of the unifying thread of temporality—and the unique challenges presented by ambiguous loss in internally displaced Greek Cypriot refugee families with a missing member." A clinical vignette highlights the different ways in which family members respond or recalibrate to identification of remains of a loved one, as well as the ways in which Cypriots create spaces where the war can be discussed. Killian's chapter also discusses the limits of the post-traumatic stress disorder label, and the effect of ambiguous loss on families. One possible means of bringing about healing and reconciliation in this type of situation is with the use of DNA testing to identify remains of loved ones. As we read drafts of this chapter, we both were conscious of other settings (such as Sri Lanka) where this is also becoming a critical part of the public discourse after reconciliation.

In "Engaging the Humanity in Front of You: Family Therapy Task Shifting in the Context of Armed Conflict," Laurie L. Charlés discusses a clinical/supervision case that took place in the humanitarian context of ongoing armed conflict in the Central African Republic. The work took place in a primary and secondary hospital while the author was working as a technical support consultant (mental health officer) for an international nongovernmental organization.

Addressed in this chapter are some of the effects on citizens' families living in the midst of armed conflict, such as repeated forced displacement, fear of persecution, and torture. This chapter also illustrates how in real time a community is transforming in the midst of war. Resources for resolving conflict and disagreement (such as respected community elders, who often serve as mediators) are often reduced or obliterated in the fracturing of infrastructure that had previously supported them. These multiple adverse extreme stressors can have unexpected and powerful effects on relationships—and may be the impetus that brings families to the attention of psychosocial and medical teams. Charlés uses personal narrative to capture to some degree the personal and professional complexity of the work in form and content, her experience working in the midst of multiple languages, with details of everyday life in the context of internal conflict in a country.

"Family Therapy In Libya: Navigating Uncharted Waters," by Malak Ben Giaber, is a personal story of a family therapy trainee who discusses her professional life in the immediate aftermath of the conflict in Libya. Speaking from the position of being "well-displaced," Ben Giaber tells us what it was like when the family therapy training course she had joined first with skepticism, then excitement, ended abruptly when competing militias increased the level of crisis in Libya. Using examples from her clinical work, which was ongoing during the training course and the reescalating conflict, Ben Giaber discusses what she felt as she heard her clients' stories at the end of the day, when she had earlier been immersed in training role-plays: "All the elements of the [family therapy] training came to life. A member of the team, the mother of a martyr of the revolution, was exhaustedly recounting how she could not handle this current war: each of her remaining two sons supported opposing factions. She said she would come home from working with IDPs [internally displaced persons] only to find her sons arguing their respective positions. She tearfully shared that she could deal with her son's death, but to have this ongoing fighting at home, a continuation of the fighting outside, was more than she could endure."

Ben Giaber's skepticism about the utility of family therapy (she is a trainee when the story of her chapter starts) is poignant and honest. Her impression speaks volumes about the differences in the ways in which family therapy practice is viewed across the globe, depending on who is doing the viewing:

... when we were told that the next training topic would be Family Therapy, I just could not make sense of it. How did that fit into humanitarian work? Was that not the new approach used especially in the United States, targeting families that were falling apart? How would that fit into Libyan society, which is very proud of the family institution, no matter how flawed it may be? How would family members come together with a complete stranger to work out issues that are highly sensitive and private? I could not imagine such a scene: a constellation of (for instance) parents, teenage girls, and their older brothers, all trying to communicate and interact in this type of context. I wondered how I would react to Family Therapy, a course I had always avoided during my master's studies. I questioned whether it was really what we needed in this type of training and whether it would "sit well" in a cultural sense.

Her questions resonate with honesty and charm, but they also reflect other discussions in the volume: What is family therapy, exactly? What is it about family therapy that makes it look one way in the United States and another way in Libya? *Does* family therapy sit well in a cultural sense? How can it do that? What about when that culture is in the midst of a revolution, with the effect that has on the mother of two fighting sons?

Gameela Samarasinghe, in her chapter, "'My Son is Alive': Is Family Therapy Appropriate for Families of the Disappeared in Sri Lanka?" explores through the experiences of Mrs. X, a mother whose son disappeared during the war, the relevance of family therapy in Sri Lanka. In so doing she describes the ordeal that families of the disappeared have gone through with the various presidential commissions while searching for the truth about their loved ones, while asking herself if family therapy could help these families. She argues that rather than family therapy, social support programs may be more appropriate for families of the disappeared in Sri Lanka. She concludes by recommending that attention be given to the impact of wider systems and social contexts on people's lives, especially with situations such as the disappearances in Sri Lanka, and that more fundamental problems at the collective level need to be addressed before those of the family and the individual.

The final chapter, "Kaleidoscopic Shifts: The Development of New Understandings as Therapists 'Go and Find Out,'" by Catalina Perdomo, Deborah Healy, Daisy Ceja, Kathryn Dunne, and Kotia Whitaker, is a joint effort by trainers and trainees in a family therapy master's program in the United States. It begins with Healey's reflections on how therapists "go and find out" how best to work with families. She compares this experience to a "kaleidoscopic shift," stating that "the smallest shift of the lens, the most delicate turn of the visual field, changes everything."

The authors then discuss in personal ways, using examples from both their family and professional lives, their faith and their experiences thus far with clients, their fears of the unknown and their future hopes for the outcome of their training. The authors' "kaleidoscopic views," offered to us as readers, illustrate their emergent understandings of family therapy across global contexts, in humanitarian settings as they have experienced and imagined them, whether witnessed on television or in the voice of the client sitting in front of them.

About This Volume

Our method for choosing contributors was a type of "snowball sampling" of those we knew doing this work in the field. Several professionals recommended the work of others they knew practicing in this area. We solicited chapter proposals from these authors. Another came on board unexpectedly, after we discovered his work in Cyprus serendipitously. In addition, although both of us have had the opportunity to meet many highly competent mental health practitioners in our work across the globe, it is Laurie who has more often met the family therapy people; we are honored that some of them have agreed to share their work in this volume.

Additionally, Laurie's work as a family therapist in the United States has brought forward the acquaintance with the work of several authors in this volume, including both Polanco and Biever and Santos, and also the unexpected beginning of the Family Therapy and Global Mental Health Student Working Group (Charlés 2015), whose months of working resulted in a chapter of their own (Perdomo et al., this volume). Each of us as coeditors has also written a chapter contribution offering perspectives or issues that we have been working on, with a view to adding a more rounded complexity to the entire set of contributions.

We have had a beautiful dilemma of language in this volume: although it is published in English and produced in an Anglophone country, the majority of the authors use other first languages, including Albanian, French, Arabic, German, and Spanish. They deliver services in languages that are not English; yet we have asked them to write about the services (which the majority of them do not deliver in English) in, yes—English.

Our editorial work has been challenged by our wish to make this dilemma overt, to keep the volume readable and friendly, and most of all, to utilize the literal complexity of voice and language as an asset to the benefit of the volume and for the reader. To our unexpected delight, this has resulted in a unique set of shifting styles of voice in each chapter; the voices here are unique in that they do not conform to one another. Even more compelling and rich, the ideas presented as sacred and certain in one chapter are contradicted in the next. The contradictions we leave to the reader to discover. We only wish to emphasize two things: the nonconforming voice is something we have made a decision to maintain, and the contradictions are completely representative of both the issues and experiences offered by the authors.

We did not expect or ask for this complexity! What we did ask was for authors to talk about their work in the field, specifically as it related to the world of family therapy. We asked them to speak to some degree about who they were, the context of the work they were describing (from the micro level of the setting to the macro level of the state indicators). They had a strict page count requirement and a few other expectations, but the manner in which they chose to tell their story was up to them. We soon observed that this lack of clear uniformity of voice—the strong uniqueness of each telling—was actually quite representative of what family therapy in global humanitarian contexts looks like on the ground. Like the chapters, the work looks different in each place; its *sounds* are different. It has an aura that native family therapists would recognize, yet its aura is unique enough in each place to completely confound the family therapist unaccustomed to the conditions or the issues in global humanitarian contexts.

We have worked hard to maintain the individual authors' unique voices as much as possible. While we did edit for clarity of ideas, coherence, and organization and English and grammar, we did not want to produce a volume that disrespected the very thing we wanted—unique voices and issues from the field—as it strengths. The power of the volume, for us, is through the voices of the authors and the originality of their contributions.

References

Anderson, H., & Goolishian, H. (1988). Human systems as linguistic systems: Evolving ideas about the implications for theory and practice. *Family Process, 27*, 371–393.

Catani, C., Schauer, E., & Neuner, F. (2008). Beyond individual war trauma: Domestic violence against children in Afghanistan and Sri Lanka. *Journal of Marital and Family Therapy, 34*(2), 165–176.

Charlés, L. (2015, July). Long live Shoufi Mafi! Family therapy in the age of global mental health. *Family Therapy Magazine*, 34–39.

Kowalcyzk, C. (2006). Liberalizing trade between large and small: The welfare from three different strategies. *Asia-Pacific Journal of Accounting & Economics, 13*, 171–179.

Landau, J., & Saul, J. (2004). Family and community resilience in response to major disaster. In F. Walsh & M. McGoldrick (Eds.), *Living beyond loss: Death in the family* (2nd ed., pp. 285–309). New York: Norton.

McDowell, T., Goessling, K., & Melendez, T. (2012). Transformative learning through international immersion: Building multicultural competence in family therapy and counseling. *Journal of Marital and Family Therapy, 38*, 365–379. doi:10.1111/j.1752-0606.2010.00209.x.

Platt, J. J. (2012). A Mexico City-based immersion education program: Training mental health clinicians for practice with Latino communities. *Journal of Marital and Family Therapy, 38*(2), 352–64. doi:10.1111/j.1752-0606.2010.00208.

Platt, J. J., & Laszloffy, T. A. (2010). *Critical patriotism: Confronting nationalism in marriage and family therapy training.* Paper presented at the annual conference of the International Family Therapy Association, Buenos Aires, Argentina.

Rivett, M. (Ed.). (2010). Looking beyond the clinic. *Journal of Family Therapy, 32*, 1–3.

Tol, W. A., Patel, V., Tomlinson, M., Baingana, F., Galappatti, A., Panter-Brick, C., & van Ommeren, M. (2011). Research priorities for mental health and psychosocial support in humanitarian settings. *PLoS Medicine, 8*(9), e1001096. doi:10.1371/journal.pmed.1001096.

Walsh, F. (2007). Traumatic loss and major disasters: Strengthening family and community resilience. *Family Process, 46*, 207–227.

Wieling, E., & Mittal, M. (2002). Expanding the horizons of marriage and family therapists: Toward global interconnectedness. *Journal of Feminist Family Therapy, 14*(1), 53–61.

Knowledge Fair Trade

Marcela Polanco

Knowledge Fair Trade

The matter I want to write about here has robbed me of many hours of sleep for the past few years. It concerns my attempts at adopting narrative therapy into a context foreign to the one in which it originated. Therefore, it relates to how I position myself, critically, as a reader of narrative therapy (White and Epston 1990).[1] This matter did not become a sleep depriving issue for me until I was able to discern that in spite of the tantalizing resonance I experienced with narrative therapy practices there was an abyss between its Australasian authors—David Epston and Michael White—and myself as a reader—a Colombian immigrant living in the U.S. The abyss was as deep as the Colombian Chicamocha Canyon, 6561 ft deep and 143 mi

---

A previous version of this paper was presented at the Therapeutic Conversations 12 Conference on May 2015, Vancouver, Canada.

I would like to give special recognition for their invaluable contributions to earlier versions of this manuscript to David Epston, Tirzah Shelton, Monte Bobele and Catalina Perdomo.

Lower case intentional.

---

[1] I have come to adopt narrative therapy as a family therapy practice that provides a context for conversations that help better discern the various effects that systems of power (colonial and otherwise) have on people's lives, infringing in our rights to fabricate life in our terms. In narrative therapy conversations, possibilities of response are rendered available hence choices to live life more attuned to our moral, ethical and aesthetical convictions rather than of the ones imposed by social, cultural and historical systems of power.

M. Polanco (✉)
Psychology Department, Our Lady of the Lake University, 411 SW 24th St, San Antonio, TX 78207, USA

long, carved by the differences in our social, historical, linguistic, political, gender, cultural and personal conditions.

The recognition of our marked differences happened after my narrative therapy in English had already turned into my lingua franca for speaking, thinking and practicing family therapy as faithfully as I could in the image and likeness of its originators. Narrative therapy had crossed over the border that separated my immigrant English from my Colombian Spanish. In my view, it did so with a "first world passport in a crisp Dolce and Gabbana suit, in first class, un-jetlagged, and unaffected by Bogotá's altitude of 8661 ft above sea level" (Polanco 2011, p. 46). In its new 'Englished,' elite status, narrative therapy became inaccessible to my speaking, thinking and practicing in my Colombian Spanish. When attempting to practice narrative therapy with Spanish speaking families my curiosity about their lives would only take form in English. Consequently, when trying to craft narrative inquiries, I was unable to access any vocabularies in Spanish. Although a bilingual, my narrative therapy had turned monolingual.

Undoubtedly, I had glossed over the many subtle and overt efforts of Epston and White to alert their readers to cultural sensitivities and humility that would keep narrative therapy from traveling around the world as a first class, global trademark. I read, or rather imported and consumed narrative therapy as a trademark, much like the trademarks of the clothes I wear and the food I eat. This led me to conclude that I had engaged in a colonizing reading of narrative therapy. Contrary to what I have come to understand as the intentions in their work, my readings of Epston and White, and the many other narrative therapists that have informed my work in English, unintentionally suffocated any possibilities of my speaking, thinking, and practicing in my Colombian Spanish, and petrified my imagination and creativity. How on earth did this happen to me given narrative therapy's philosophy of social justice? Well, this may very well had to do with something beyond narrative therapy's radical epistemological and philosophical intentions of resistance against the very same practices I engaged with when reading it.

For the French, literary theorist Roland Barthes (1977), a text contains multiple layers of meanings that depend on the impressions of the reader instead of the passions or intentions of the writer. For Barthes, the author produces a text and the reader explains it. The power of interpretation lies on the reader rather than on what he called—the Author-God. Hence, he proclaimed, metaphorically speaking, the death of the single interpretative power of the Author-God of a text. Although, I am a bit critical of his proposal of giving interpretative power only to the reader rather than sustaining a dialogical, interpretative partnership between reader and writer, his proposal may shed some light here on my predicament. The power of interpretation of a reader could turn any texts by the founders of narrative therapy, Epston or White, which have the intentions to be anti-colonial, into colonial texts depending on how the reader reads them and on the reader's historical, social, political and cultural conditions. In retrospect, the contextual conditions of my first readings had me engaged in a colonizing reading of narrative therapy.

More recently, I have been repositioning myself to find alternatives that allow for a decolonizing reading of foreign knowledge, consequently leading me to considerations of constructing my renewed, local, more culturally suitable versions of narrative therapy. I accessed these alternatives through a de-colonial translation of narrative therapy into my Colombian and Latin American terms. This translation required me to let go of Epston and White's terms to pick up my own, together with the ones of Latin American authors who share similar anti-colonial concerns and who are intimately connected to the vicissitudes of my cultures.

Due to limits of space, I am here only discussing the problematization of the internationalization of professional knowledge. This is, as relevant to narrative therapy or family therapy training across borders, inadvertently engaging with a colonizing agenda that result in the faithful adoption of its practices into local cultures as the only legitimate alternatives. I hope to raise a critical perspective to be considered by family therapists when training and practicing in global contexts. This is by cautioning the reader on the importance of situating family therapy theories in the euroamerican geographical and political contexts in which they belong along with their values, traditions and intentions, making visible their foreignness and potential intentions to domesticate or suffocate if not received critically. Rendering foreignness visible may open space for the reader/audience to imagine their own transformative local production of knowledge outside the euroamerican paradigms. The matter of the renewal of more suitable, de-colonial alternatives of narrative family therapy practices I am documenting elsewhere.

Among the alternatives that resulted in my repositioning as a reader I am introducing below one of a multi-lateral fair trade of knowledge across cultures, which I believe contributes to maintain the integrity of all contributors. This may be of relevance, particularly to therapists who self-identify outside of the euro American paradigms. In my case, it has led me to rethink, reimagine and reinvent my former euro-american family therapy training into a practice more so in tune with my cultural locations as a Colombian immigrant in the U.S., working with families of Latin American heritages. My Colombian oral storytelling traditions, magical-realist's worldviews, and de-colonial ethics, for example, have found their way into my therapeutic conversations, which lead me to ask questions that would raise the eyebrows of my euro-american colleagues when, for example, I become curious about how someone's heart changes colors and tastes differently under various circumstances of their lives. The matter of the renewal of more suitable, de-colonial alternatives of narrative family therapy practices, however, I am documenting elsewhere.

While my experience here relates in particular to narrative therapy, it very well applies to the field of family therapy which is informed to a great degree by western European and anglo North American worldviews. For that I will start with a discussion of the contextual conditions that led me to engage in a colonizing reading of narrative therapy in the first place given my historical, social, political, economical and cultural conditions as a narrative therapy reader.

My Historical and Cultural Conditions as a Reader

My name is Marcela Polanco bejarano. It is written in small letters to emphasize that the life that it carries does not stay put, nor does it hold aspirations to claim any authority of the proper conventions of the classes of names. My first name came to me on account of a temporary memory lapse by my mother. At the time of registering my name, she had forgotten that the name she and my father had chosen to secure me a good life was Gisela, not Marcela—also a name of Italian origin. According to my family's history, my paternal last name has its origins during the times of Colombia's systematic colonization by Spain. Around the late 1800s two Polanco brothers from Spain settled in Tolima, west central area of Colombia, in the land of the Pijao aboriginal communities. This is the land where my father's family lived for many generations and some still do. My maternal last name, Bejarano, also has Spanish origins. Specifically, it comes from the Bejarano Jewish families that were exiled from Spain in the 1500s. They settled in Muisca territory where I was born and raised. My cousin Elsa and I have no doubts that beyond our aboriginal and European heritages, Africana blood also runs through our veins but we have no record of it.

My mixed heritage defines me as a mestiza. Therefore, as a mestiza, my body represents the battlegrounds of the oppressor and the oppressed and the colonizer and the colonized. My mestiza body yearns to transgress such duality by aspiring to a yet unknown postcolonial existence. In the Spanish colonial system of racial hierarchy defined to determine the degree of purity of one's blood and to subsequently determine the conferral of people's rights, mestizos and mestizas were lower in the social, political, economic and social continuum. Our rights to humanity-worthiness were beneath that of the Colombian-born Spaniards or Criollos, and over that of the African and Aboriginal communities. After the so-called independence from the Spanish colonization, mestizos and mestizas became the majority and the dominant group. We strived to represent ourselves as close as possible to possessing a Spanish heritage by dispossessing ourselves from any afra or aboriginal traditions, language or worldviews; although of course we proceeded to take possession of their lands. Mestizos and mestizas acquired the language of our colonizers, their western worldview, their god, their justice system, their values and their violent relationship with nature. We denied representations of anything other than western eurocentric views.

Our colonization resulted in our internalization of the European colonizing gaze to continue their ethnocidal project. When looking at ourselves through euro-christian eyes, however, we grew suspicious of the degree of our own humanity, striving for the impossible—the purity of the white skin. We attempted to whiten our consciousness and worldviews by uprooting our traditions for the salvation of our souls according to their god. Our colonization resulted in becoming colonizers to one another in the image and likeness of our colonizer. I don't know any more atrocious and despicable effects of colonization than the turning against one another to further replicate the inhumane solitude of such an act; or, according to the Martinique-born Afro Caribbean revolutionary and philosopher, Fanon (1961/2001), to systematically deny another, depriving them of qualities of humanity.

The Second Arrival of Columbus

I am not necessarily writing here about a history that took place 500 years ago even though it may have started back then. I am writing about the history of our colonization that is alive and well in the early 21st century. Social hierarchies according to which rights are conferred to people remain. For example, I am part of the approximated 27 % of colombians with access to higher education; the 7 % whom had access to a bilingual education, and the 2 % who completed a degree as a bilingual. In my better-situated conditions, which result in worsening the conditions of millions of others, I earn about 10 times more than 67 % of the 47.662.000 colombians, with a 12 % difference between women earning less than men.

Shiva (2011), physicist, author and environmental activist from India, said it best; "we are experiencing now the second coming of Columbus," this is, "a more secular version of the same project of colonization…" (p. 158). In Colombia, for example, the second coming of Columbus arrived on July 14th 1995 as the first McDonald's©[2] fast food chain store opened its doors. They opened their first restaurant in the exclusive mall Andino, located in a privileged neighborhood north of Bogotá. At long last Colombia was worthy of a McDonald's©, some of us thought. It was a faithful replica of a U.S. McDonald's©. There was absolutely nothing Colombian about it. Even the staff were strategically recruited for that purpose. While Colombians, they had the most Anglo traits amongst us.

At the time, I was working as an organizational psychologist in human resources at a large multinational food company in Bogotá. My colleagues and I—all part of the 2 % of bilingual professionals graduated from the same top private universities in the country and now working at better-paid multinational companies—were eagerly awaiting its arrival. We wanted to experience a piece of the enchanting American Dream. Despite our plans, however, we were not able to make it on the opening day, nor on the weeks that followed. The line to get in was outrageously long and tangled up like the arteries of our bodies that were about to be challenged by their Mcfood.

McDonald's© arrival came 4 years after President Gaviria declared an open economy in 1990. In only one year, 10 of its restaurants were opened with an investment of 85 million dollars. In no other country did it grow as fast as in Colombia. McDonald's© strategy of capital expansion is only one example of the

---

[2]Among other things, McDonald's© is one of the largest companies in the world that acts aggressively against any attempts by their employees to organize themselves into trade unions.

agenda of the second coming of Columbus. This agenda started to take shape at the end of the Second World War. It promoted a neoliberal modern ideal of development, serving as a context for the development and consumption of knowledge.[3] I will continue to outline it here, drawing heavily from the work of the colombian anthropologist, Escobar (2007).

A Neoliberal Market for Knowledge

On January 20th of 1949, U.S. President Truman (1964) announced to the world in his inaugural address his concept of fair trade to resolve the problems of the world in underdeveloped countries, introducing the word *underdeveloped* for the first time:

> ...More than half the people of the world are living in conditions approaching misery. Their food is inadequate. They are victims of disease. [Note here, however, that who is speaking is the president of the country that invented McDonald's© and that has the highest rates of obesity-caused mortality in the world]. Their economic life is primitive and stagnant. Their poverty is a handicap and a threat both to them and to more prosperous areas. For the first time in history, humanity possesses the knowledge and skill to relieve the suffering of these people. The United States is pre-eminent among nations in the development of industrial and scientific techniques... I believe that we should make available to peace-loving peoples the benefits of our store of technical knowledge in order to help them realize their aspirations for a better life....What we envisage is a program of development based on the concepts of democratic fair-dealing...Greater production is the key to prosperity and peace. And the key to greater production is a wider and more vigorous application of modern scientific and technical knowledge (para. 45).

While proposed as a democratic fair dealing, it seems a rather unilateral one, involving naming others' misery and poverty for the justification of the application of the neoliberal modern agenda of scientific and technical knowledge of the U.S. and prosper countries. Colombia got word of these grandiose ideas, even 50 years after. Despite our handicapped, primitive and stagnant conditions, although questionably peace-loving peoples given our international representation of drug trade (with prosperous countries), we learned to realize that our aspirations for a better life were worth standing in line for weeks to obtain the so desired key to unlock our stagnation into prosperity at any cost. Never mind that such a key comes at times in the form of a big clown dressed in red and yellow. But only then could we consume the key of modern greatness that humanity possesses to relieve our suffering and to realize our aspirations of life because we do not seem to have the capabilities to do so ourselves.

---

[3]See John Williamson's (2004) work on the Washington Consensus referring to economic policies by Washington D.C.-based institutions to solve the world's crisis, with particular interest in Latin America, including the International Monetary Fund, the World Bank and the U.S. Treasury Department.

This rhetoric spread worldwide. It created the necessary conditions in countries referred to as underdeveloped, like Colombia, to reproduce the characteristics required for neoliberal development. This is the kind of development of industrialization, urbanization, technification of agriculture, fast growing material production and life status, and adoption of modern cultural values of education (Escobar 2007) and knowledge. These are the conditions for the realization of the American Dream trademark in almost every single corner of the world. According to Iranian, Rahnema (1986) poverty, illiteracy and hunger have never been so profitable sources for industrialized countries—in the name of progress and development.

Fast forwarding fifty years after Truman's speech, the World Bank (1999) took a look at development problems across the globe.[4,5] In their study, they took a look at development this time from the perspective of knowledge. They concluded that "poor" countries differ from "rich" countries because they have less knowledge. The production of knowledge, they considered, is too expensive. That is the reason it asserts why most of the production of knowledge is generated in industrial countries. In turn, they concluded that developing countries do not need to reinvent the wheel. Instead of recreating existing knowledge, poor countries have the option of acquiring and adapting knowledge that is already available in countries that are richer. Acquiring knowledge for poor countries would then involve accessing and adopting available knowledge through a free trade arrangement, foreign capital investment, and assuring that the poor have access (de Souza Silva 2008).

Now, what counts as legitimate knowledge in the modern development agenda of the World Bank that it is only produced within the capabilities of the wealth of industrialized countries—wealth accumulated at the expense of third world countries? What are the implications of representing us through their discursive hegemony of "development" as "poor" and "underdeveloped"? And, is their proposed free trade agreement yet another unilateral strategy to continue stripping our resources in exchange for the industrialized knowledge of rich countries?[6]

Knowledge, in the era of the second Columbus, has become a vehicle for the proliferation of the neoliberal modern development agenda, particularly through its professionalization. It became the institutionalizing means to organize, validate and disseminate development, and ways of being, globally through academia and

---

[4]The World Bank is supposed to be one of the most democratic organizations that lend humanitarian aid around the world, together with the World Trade Organization, and the International Monetary Fund. However, they are run by a board of directors of only 6 of its 188 member countries, none of them elected by vote. None of the 6 directors represent countries from Latin America, Africa or the Middle East. They are China, France, United Kingdom, Japan, Germany, and, of course, United States.

[5]For a more recent perspective on development, see the United Nations agenda on the Sustainable Development Goals agreement released on 2015.

[6]These questions could very well apply to the production of knowledge within the field of family therapy. What counts as legitimate practices? Are only evidence-based, published models of practice what counts for training and practice? Are family therapists adopting similar positions as the World Bank to determine what counts as billable and legitimate?

scientific research. From the geopolitics of knowledge, in the colonial system of classification of the second coming of Columbus, the legitimation of knowledge, language and identity is determined by a geographical place and origin (Mignolo 2005/2012). What counts as legitimate today comes in certain languages and from certain places—For example, it comes in the language in which I am writing this manuscript, it is white, patriarchal, heterosexual, and comes with a first world trademark seal of approval.

The rhetoric of the arrival of the new Columbus, once again, has stripped our capabilities to produce legitimate knowledge from which to raise consciousness about our own conditions of oppression. Our double internalized colonization has convinced us that the neoliberal agenda of development is what we ought to aspire for, and therefore, to achieve it, we ought to stand in line as long as it takes to obtain it. We ought to access their sacred industrialized knowledge to consume it while we become consumed by it. No matter if it this is done at the expense of the exploitation of our local cultures, women, identity, history and land. We are defined as poor, ill, fragile, vulnerable and stagnant therefore we must be rescued by the first world dressed in red and yellow. In Shiva's (2011) terms: "Five hundred years ago, it was enough to be a non-Christian culture to lose all claims and rights. Five hundred years after Columbus, it is enough to be a non-Western culture with a distinctive worldview and diverse knowledge system to lose all claims and rights. The humanity of others was blanked out then and […] [our] intellect is being blanked out now (p. 160). The new Columbus has arrived with a clear agenda. Shiva (2011) puts it very clearly:

> The principle of effective occupation by Christian princes has been replaced by effective occupation by the transnational corporations supported by modern-day rules…The duty to incorporate slaves into Christianity has been replaced by the duty to incorporate local and national economies into the global marketplace, and to incorporate non-western systems of knowledge into the reductionism of commercialized Western science and technology. (p. 151)

The neoliberal, modern, colonial agenda of development seeks to eradicate the differences among our cultures.

In Colombia, I suspect that it may be us, the 27 % with access to higher education and the 2 % with access to bilingual education that later govern the other 73 %, whom might be at the core of replicating the colonial neoliberal agenda of development. With our chests full of air and our chins up, some of us display in our professional or academic offices our doctoral degree diplomas from European or North American universities. We do so as a symbol of development and of the realization of our dreams of progress and civilization. And, perhaps, seeking recognition for the hard work it required some of us to obtain it, while rolling up our trademark, ironed sleeves when seating comfortably at our mahogany desks to type away the world on our Apple© computers, only at the expense of few hours of sleep. Although, I wonder if a Wayuu, indigenous woman in Colombia, who has been caught in the crossfire of Colombia's civil war between paramilitary, guerilla, drug traffickers and government forces would share the same idea of hard work.

Our diplomas confirm that we, the poor, peace-loving peoples have gained the key to access the legitimate knowledge of the "rich" so that the World Bank can be at peace with itself. We have obtained it first hand as close as possible to a replica of the English, patriarchal, white, heterosexual, first world knowledge. Only now do we have the capability to overcome our stagnation and to solve our suffering. Therefore, we can proceed to strip off our mochilas[7] and ruanas[8] so we can bring the scientific, professional knowledge back to our country, now in our crisp Dolce and Gabbana suits, in first class, un-jetlagged and unaffected by Bogotá's altitude of 8661 ft above sea level. We do so for the ignorant, poor, underdeveloped, stagnant and illiterate fellow colombian to no longer be required to wait in line for it. What we don't know, however, is that our well-intentioned and better-situated actions are, once again, further replicating the worse colonizing act: The compromising of our own liberation by turning against one another.

Subaltern Knowledges

Our first world therapy diplomas turned us blind and deaf to the real sabios and sabias—the subaltern wise. They are the ones whom have known how to recognize, resist and oppose, with their lives, if necessary, the euro-christian rhetoric of salvation and the first-world rhetoric of neoliberal modern development, no matter how cute and charming the clown who delivers it may be. By the subaltern wise I am referring to the 102 Aboriginal communities in Colombian territory, with 68 different languages and 292 dialects. They are still facing extinction but have survived the arrival of many Columbus-es clothed in various ways over the past 500 years. I am also referring to the 4 million of afra/o Colombians who remind us that resistance is possible and that colonization is unstable; and to the 7.1 million campesinas/os whom have always known the value of our land. Only they, who have invented many wheels long before the World Bank even existed, will help us overcome our colonial education of blindness; only they will help us see that our diplomas turned us poor.

Unlearning neoliberal development may lead us to our decolonization so we could imagine a different Colombia, Latin America, Africa and Asia. I agree with Escobar (2007) when considering that this will not take place in professional academic circles. Nor will it happen in the offices of the World Bank or the scientific journals of Tier 1 universities in the U.S. or the U.K. It will take place, instead, in a de-colonial project based on the trafficking of the local interpretations of everyday life, where the subaltern engages in practices of restitutions of their

---

[7]Handcrafted indigenous backpacks.

[8]Handcrafted, wool, poncho-like garment wore by native Muiscas.

land, identities, relationships and cultural meanings and productions. Unbeknownst to the World Bank, the subaltern has had a voice and the subaltern has spoken even though the audibility of their voices in academic circles has been barely heard (Escobar 2007).

Fair Trade

So, what about narrative therapy (or any other family therapy frameworks)? As a perspective that traffics in the periphery of conventional practices, seeking to interrogate the effects of the production of life when following first world, neoliberal, diagnostic, eurocentric parameters, I believe that it presents itself as an important contributor and ally. Narrative therapists often situate at the forefront the historical, social, cultural and relational contexts of the authorship of knowledge, exploring a multiplicity of knowledges, particularly from the subaltern formerly displaced by a problem embedded in neoliberal systems of power.

To enter into a multi-lateral fair trade agreement with narrative therapy required me to reverse my earlier training that resulted in the English monopoly of my practice. Instead of continuing my attempts at bringing narrative therapy into my Colombian Spanish unjetlagged, I had to delink (Mignolo 2005/2012) from its practices to facilitate instead a fair, reciprocal inter-cultural—rather than inter-national—intellectual and practical trade agreement. Only then an exchange between two legitimate contributors could be facilitated; and hybrid de-colonial options could be conceived to inform one another about our local "respective life support systems" (Rahnema 1986, p. 44)—respecting each other's Chicamocha-canyon-like-abyss-differences in solidarity while doing so.

Such agreement presented itself to me as a challenge at first, however. What local life support systems, claims and rights from my colombian culture did I have to bring to the table to establish an alliance with narrative therapy for a decolonial project? None whatsoever. My knowledge in Spanish came from my training in Colombia, which had already undergone intellectual colonization by the unilateral internationalizing trends of the euro-american disciplines of psychiatry and psychology, currently being followed by family therapy. After psychiatry, psychology settled in my country and I had access to through Skinner, Pavlov and Freud. Psychology practices were founded on euro-american evidence-based criteria, with techniques that monitor the development of human behavior from stagnation toward progress on the realization of aspirations of first world happiness, health, and prosperity.

According to Afra and Afro Colombians Libia Grueso, Leyla Arroyo and Carlos Rosero from the *Organization of Black Communities from the Pacific* in Colombia (see Escobar 2007), it is our task to advance local formulations and implementations of new social and cultural alternatives that would inform our therapeutic work, prior to any engagements of fair dealings with foreign therapy productions. These local formulations, however, are not about literal translations or adaptations of foreign therapeutic theories into my Colombian Spanish. Adaptations of narrative or family therapy maintain the same expansionist patterns of first world, global criteria to make it readily accessible for local consumption. I had actually attempted this kind of adaptation of narrative practice, unknowingly confirming the global systems of power I have represented here.

Instead, a decolonial project applied to therapy practice departs from subaltern *local* formulations of social, cultural and personal transformation translated into *local* political, cultural and social alternatives to invent new options for practice rooted in the domestic. These would destabilize dominant, scientific ways of knowing in the current mental health field i.e. diagnostic knowledge: and would contribute to the liberation of our imagination and creativity in our practices, in defense of cultural difference. Local subaltern therapeutic formulations could draw from the relentless Latin American grass-roots, social, historical and cultural movements (Escobar 2007) such as the Mexican indigenous Zapatista Movement, the Brazilian Movimiento Sin Tierra, The Cocalero Movement of campesina/os in Colombia, The Mothers of the Plaza de Mayo in Argentina, the Arpillera women movement in Chile, and other Latin American feminists, campesina/os, chicana/os, working class and black movements. These movements tell us that "we are much more than we are told" (Galeano 2013, para. 17), tradition in Latin America has not vanished and global trends of development have not fully and successfully arrived (Canclini 1990). Not only these offer material for our imagination to construct local therapeutic formulations to facilitate unsuffering processes. They also, remind us that we are capable of creating our own life-support-systems-based therapeutic movements than strictly waiting in line to consume formulations produced and delivered to us from evidence-based euro-american professional journals; even when their foreignness is disguised in our own native language.

Other options for therapeutic local formulations that I consider represent life support systems of everyday life in my Colombian cultures come from resistance and transgression of modern development via magical-realist forms. These are embedded in the mix of our Africana, Aboriginal and European heritages as serve as interpretative frames everywhere in our everyday lives García Márquez (1980–1984). The work of colombian anthropologists Pinzón and Suárez Prieto (1992) illustrates this. They visited 15 psychiatric hospitals in Bogotá over a period of three years. They learned that 32 % of working class patients, emphatically argued, based on their local knowledge, that they were not crazy. Instead, from their magical-realist worldviews, they were under a spell. They were violently put into hospitals against their will. They developed strategies to confront the blind and deaf official western treatments of the hospital. They created and ran groups of opposition to legitimate their healing practices. In their view, only *curandeas/os* would know how to help their circumstances instead of the official professionals of the hospital. They were the only ones with the appropriate knowledge for such a task. Therapeutic practices informed by culturally appropriate knowledge dignify and legitimize local knowledge.

Commentaries

An inter-cultural fair trade agreement of narrative and family therapy knowledge could benefit from decolonial strategies that protect the cultural integrity of the therapist, the consultant and their communities, within their respective historical, social, cultural, political, etc. conditions. It could facilitate the restitution of our rights, as therapists and consultants, to name our practices as much as our social sufferings and unsufferings in our own terms, when resisting the universal euro-american persuasive promises of Christian salvation, civilization, progress, and modern neoliberal development that have not skipped the mental health field. A fair trade agreement emphasizes that modern euro-american knowledge, like family therapy, is not to be eradicated, however. Not only would that be impossible, naive and limiting but it would convey the same dangerous, single, universal paradigm (Mignolo 2005/2012). Instead, a fair trade project involves redefining both the content of family therapy knowledge by local practitioners informed by local practices; and the terms of the current unilateral global and international training of family therapy in *other* countries around the world. Unilateral trades of knowledge ought to consider bilateral or multi-lateral agreements of training and practice supported by solidarity, cultural humility and mutual respect to be different no matter how tantalizing foreign criteria may be. This would support a kind of alliance that eradicates colonialism not only in the territories of our practices but in our lands and our consciousness (Fanon 1961/2001). And for this to happen, according to Peruvian sociologist, Quijano (1990), as therapists, "we ought to stop being what we have not been, and what we will never be, and what we have to be… we ought to stop being strictly modern" (p. 37).

References

Barthes, R. (1977). *Image, music text* (S. Heath, Trans.). London, UK: Fontana Press. (Original work published 1977).
de Souza Silva, J. (2008). *La geopolítica del conocimiento y la gestión de procesos de innovación en la época histórica emergente*. Unpublished.
Escobar, A. (2007). *La invención del tercer mundo: La construcción y deconstrucción del desarrollo*. Caracas, Venezuela: La Fundación Editorial el perro y la rana.
Fanon, F. (1961/2001). *The wretched of the earth* (C. Farrington, Trans.). London, UK: Penguin Books. (Original work published 1961).
Galeano, E. (2013, July 23). Eduardo Galeano: My greater fear is that we are all suffering from amnesia. *The Guardian*. Retrieved from http://www.theguardian.com/books/2013/jul/23/eduardo-galeano-children-days-interview.
García Canclini, N. (1990). *Culturas híbridas, estrategias para entrar y salir de la modernidad*. Mexico City, Mexico: Grijalbo.
García Márquez, G. (1980–1984). El amargo encanto de la máquina de escribir [The bittersweet enchantment of the typewriter]. In *Notas de Prensa 1980–1984* (pp. 362–365). Bogota, Colombia: Editorial Norma.

Mignolo, W. D. (2005/2012). *La idea de América Latina: La herida colonial y la opción decolonial* (S. Jawerbaum & J. Barba, Trans.). Barcelona, Spain: Editorial Gedisa. (Original work published 2005).

Pinzón, C. E., & Suárez Prieto, R. (1992). *Las mujeres lechuza: Historia, cuerpo y brujería en Boyacá*. Colombia: Serie Amerindia.

Polanco, m. (2011). Autoethnographic means to the end of a decolonizing translation. *Journal of Systemic Therapies, 30*(3), 42–56.

Quijano, A. (1990). Estética de la Utopía. *David y Goliath, 57*, 34–38.

Rahnema, M. (1986). Under the banner of development. *Seeds of Change, 1*(2), 37–46.

Shiva, V. (2011). *Biopiracy: The plunder of nature and knowledge*. New Delhi, India: Natraj Publishers.

Truman, H. (1964). *Public Papers of the Presidents of the United States, Harry S. Truman*. Washington, DC: Government Printing Office. Retrieved from http://www.trumanlibrary.org/publicpapers/index.php?pid=1030&st=inaugural&st1=.

White, M., & Epston, D. (1990). *Narrative means to therapeutic ends*. New York, NY: W. W. Norton.

Williamson, J. (2004). *A short history of the Washington consensus*. Paper presented at the Fundación CIDOB conference from the Washington consensus towards a new global governance. Barcelona, Spain.

World Bank. (1999). *World development report 1998/1999: Knowledge for development*. Washington, DC: Oxford University Press.

Humanitarianism, Colonization, and/or Collaboration? Working Together in Uganda and the United States

Teresa McDowell and Paschal Kabura

Introduction

On the broadest level, humanitarian principles of humanity, neutrality, impartiality, and independence (Barnett and Weiss 2008) are congruent with our work as family therapists and counselors. From this frame we might see ourselves practicing small acts of humanitarianism in the intimate context of our daily work. We spend our lives helping others live better, more satisfying and fulfilling lives. We typically respect each individual's and family's right to self-determination. We are expected to be impartial—treating all others with respect and putting equal effort into each person's care. Most of us engage in the profession in spite of the pay, rather than for the pay.

When we hear the term *humanitarian*, however, we typically think of actions taken on a large scale—one group with greater resources helping another group in dire need. We think of providing relief to strangers during times of war or famine. More recently, as humanitarian agendas have expanded, we may think of offering emotional support after natural disasters or even engaging in the work of international human rights (Barnett and Weiss 2008).

Humanitarianism sounds simple. What action could be more clear or obvious than feeding someone who is hungry? Helping someone who is in pain? In reality, humanitarianism is complex and often contradictory. Humanitarian-based foreign aid is often part of a larger colonial agenda that maintains the power of the high-resource countries while primarily benefitting the most powerful in low-resource countries, coinciding with or becoming what Barnett and Weiss (2008, p. 3) described as "part of the grand strategies of many powerful states." Mental health

---

T. McDowell (✉)
Lewis & Clark Graduate School of Education and Counseling, Portland, USA
e-mail: teresamc@lclark.edu

P. Kabura
Bishop Magambo Counsellor Training Institute, Fort Portal, Uganda

training and community interventions in high-need areas of the world are no exception. These interventions are often financially unsustainable and impose Western, colonizing frameworks of mental health and recovery.

We have been deeply engaged in working together as counseling and family therapy educators across Uganda and the United States in support of international cross training for the past decade. More recently we have been engaging in local mental health–based humanitarian interventions in communities in Western Uganda. While our work does not fall within the strict definition of humanitarianism, it crosses over into humanitarian action and is informed by humanitarian ideals. We continuously consider the ethics of humanitarianism and the power of colonizing processes as we collaborate, share field knowledge, and redistribute resources across the global North and global South. The questions we have been asking ourselves and which also guide this chapter include, "How do we engage in counseling-based humanitarianism across contexts shaped by unjust global power dynamics without compromising equity, fairness, and justice? Without participating in a world order that promotes colonization by those who have the means to fund humanitarian projects?" In other words, "How do we engage in truly collaborative humanitarianism?"

Placing Our Work in Socio-Political and Historical Context

To work collaboratively, we need to understand how countries across which we are working (and the relationships between them) are situated in the global context. This includes political, economic, and societal systems within and across national borders. It also includes our histories in relationship to each other. We must continuously position our relationships within social context, from the broadest level of project planning and delivery to the minutest person-to-person interactions.

In our case, this context encompasses the history between the European, North American, and African continents, including the Scramble for Africa, the slave trade, and colonial rule, as well as the contemporary effects of global capitalism. Western frameworks such as environmental determinism and the view of modern progress as a linear advancement of technology have justified colonial attitudes and actions "on behalf of" African nations seen as primitive and unable to judge what is best for themselves. These narratives impact humanitarian action, which is further influenced by narratives of victims of disaster as being helpless (Barnett and Weiss 2008).

Journeying Together with Caution

We recognize that through our work together in Uganda we are both potential agents of colonization. Paschal received his professional training and doctorate in the United States and began the first counselor training program in rural Uganda.

Teresa is U.S.-born and trained. We find our work together to be fraught with ethical dilemmas based on global power dynamics. For example, Teresa's work in the global South has promoted her career in the global North. Our research in Uganda is typically published in journals in the global North, and our unequal access to travel and entry into each other's countries as well as the relative value of Ugandan shillings to U.S. dollars creates lopsided opportunities for faculty and students at both institutions.

Aware of the dangers of the colonizing tendencies that often infect humanitarian work, we have embraced our collaboration with caution. We met in 2005 at the Bishop Magambo Counsellor Training Institute (BMCTI), which Paschal founded near the Rwenzori Mountains in Fort Portal. Fort Portal is in the Western region, Toro subregion, and Kabarole District of Uganda, not far from the Democratic Republic of Congo. We toured the Western counseling rooms and indigenous counseling huts before having a lively discussion about our work across continents. This short visit has in ten years resulted in what will soon be four international trainings, talks at international conferences, and ongoing transnational research among students and staff at BMCTI and Lewis & Clark College (L&C). Redistributing economic resources is in our case foundational to humanitarian action, leading L&C graduate students and BMCTI faculty to create a nonprofit organization that supports staff development and capacity building at BMCTI along with on-the-ground, local humanitarian-based community interventions (for example, It Takes a Village Uganda http://itvuganda.wix.com/itvuganda#!about-us/cjg9).

Humanitarianism, Space, and Place

Humanitarianism can be understood as occurring within and across specific spaces and places at particular times. Humanitarian acts often occur as a result of damage to physical space that renders an area dangerous, inhospitable, and/or unsupportive of human life, for example, earthquakes, drought, or armed conflict. Most of those living where dangerous events occur are space-bound. That is, they are unable to simply move to safer environments that are more conducive to human life. If they do flee or are evacuated they face great loss and often enter new spaces that are only marginally livable, for example, refugee camps or shelters. It is typically those with the fewest resources who are the most vulnerable and space-bound; those with the greatest resources have the greatest access to mobility (McDowell 2015). Consider the disaster in New Orleans as an example. Those who were rendered most space-bound prior to Hurricane Katrina—those with the fewest resources and least amount of social and cultural capital (Bourdieu 1986)—were in far greater danger, were last to be rescued, and lost far more than those with the greatest economic resources, who lived in the safest locations and who were prioritized for evacuation (Thiede and Brown 2013).

Place has great meaning for those who inhabit specific spaces. Wars that lead to the need for humanitarian intervention are often based on struggles to define, secure, and/or inhabit places of importance. These places often hold spiritual or existential meaning, as with, for example, the Israeli-Palestinian conflict. Forced exodus often means loss of such places, an example being the U.S. removal of Native Americans from places of meaning within spaces that supported life to desolate reservation spaces without history, spiritual meaning, or environmental sustenance.

Human needs for safety, social interaction, personal space, and privacy are often suspended during and after events that call for humanitarian action. For example, the genocide in Rwanda interrupted daily social interactions between those who had been neighbors in shared communities. Homes were invaded; personal space and privacy were rendered meaningless. The ultimate invasion of personal space and lack of safety resulted in death for approximately eight hundred thousand Rwandans. The world stepped back and watched as one country after another refused assistance. Now, postgenocide victims are struggling to cope with living in the same spaces in which they were raped and tortured, and watched friends and family lose their lives (Schimmel 2010); their sense of place is permanently altered. There is ample evidence that our geography—where we live and under what conditions—deeply affects our mental health and relational well-being (Hudson 2012).

It is into these spaces, in which the security of place has been shattered, that humanitarians often enter. The boundaries that once surrounded these spaces become more permeable; outsiders are invited or otherwise find their way into provide aid. The presence of outsiders with needed resources creates temporary shared space or what can be thought of as humanitarian borderlands, where boundaries overlap between cultures, nations, global class divides, and professions.

Borderlands are more than shared spaces. They are often spaces in which ways of living and doing are in contest, resources are unequally shared, and access to what is considered basic to human rights is unevenly distributed (Anzaldua 2007). Mechanisms of marginalization, exclusion, oppression, and resistance that existed before the need for assistance are still present and can be exacerbated via the entry of yet another (powerful) group with culturally-bound helping agendas. Humanitarianism in its purest form assumes that space can be temporarily occupied with a neutral agenda of helping those who are suffering space-bound trauma (e.g., war, famine, natural disaster). Those who come into shared spaces with humanitarian intentions, however, have greater resources and power to influence those in need, who are typically in highly vulnerable situations (Barnett and Weiss 2008). Humanitarian efforts to help counsel and care for others often occur through non-governmental organizations (NGOs), which may mirror processes of colonial, power-over relationships.

Humanitarian aid offered through NGOs can fail to uphold historical principles of humanitarianism: humanity, neutrality, impartiality, and independence. NGO activity should not be confused with humanitarianism in its purest form; however, in practice the boundaries between humanitarian intentions and the activities of NGOs have become increasingly blurred (Barnett and Weiss 2008). Viewing aid to

Uganda through a neocolonial lens, and considering the outcomes of ground interventions offered by NGOs and/or groups defined as humanitarian, unveils problems associated with many Western mental health interventions.

Example: Training to Help Child Soldiers of the Lord's Resistance Army

Aid money is often poured into Western-tailored mental health workshops and interventions without consulting or using local resources or counselors. Local Ugandan counselors are not included in the decision making about what is best for their own communities. When they do lead projects they are often bound by specific funder agendas such as women in development or preparing single mothers for the workforce. Local people are typically hired for lesser roles, which furthers the perception that they are less competent and valuable than outsiders. Funders arrive on site driving big cars, and then stay in nice houses and decide what they want locals to do. This is all done without a sophisticated understanding of unintended consequences or long-term effects. For example, an NGO recently came to Uganda after securing approximately one million Euros to rehabilitate child soldiers of the Lord's Resistance Army. The NGO sent a team of experts to manage the project. They had a fleet of sport-utility vehicles, lived luxurious lives in Kampala, drove to the rural north to conduct a few workshops, and even offered sitting allowances to the participants, who were considered uninformed. The training was not only Western based (read, colonizing) in content and delivery, but also set up an unsustainable expectation that future trainings in Uganda would not only be free but would pay participants a fee for attending. This undermined local training efforts, which are viewed as substandard without the (colonial) authority associated with professionals from the global North, yet which require participants to pay attendance fees.

Example: Unintended Consequences of Aid to Child-Headed Families

A recent study near Fort Portal in the Kabarole District revealed the importance of NGO contributions to the welfare of child-headed families. In their study of twenty child-headed families, Kipp et al. (2010) found that five of the families had NGO support. These families were able to eat three times a day (in contrast to a maximum of twice a day in nonsupported families), as well as to attend school and have other basic needs met. However, the findings also drew attention to some unintended consequences of NGO funding. The children without support were not aware of any available support or how to access it. Children with support became less resourceful, reached out less often to extended support systems, and became dependent on stable income from outside sources. More importantly, funded children were frequently targeted and discriminated against out of envy. Children told stories of mistreatment by extended family and neighbors due to their NGO-supported economic advantage. While the NGOs' efforts to directly fund child-headed families were admirable and helpful at the most basic level of survival, they created a system of privilege and marginalization that could possibly have been avoided if local experts had been involved in decision making relative to distribution of funds.

Toward Collaborative Humanitarianism

Given the uneven territory of humanitarianism—the very nature of one group having resources the other needs and the imbalance of power that that dynamic creates—we wonder if it is truly possible to engage in what we are defining here as collaborative humanitarianism. In some ways this reflects the dilemma we face daily in our work with clients: to provide help while respecting the expertise and independence of those with whom we work.

Example: Community Intervention into Domestic Violence

During L&C and BMCTI joint family therapy trainings in Uganda we have routinely spent time talking about and sharing resources on domestic violence. This is a problem we share across cultural and national contexts. We explore the cycle of abuse and the ways in which it plays out in each of our culturally diverse contexts. Participants chose this as a topic for a narrative theater exercise during one of our trainings, highlighting the relevance of domestic violence intervention in their local community.

The growing awareness of the cycle of abuse that emerged from our collaboration prompted BMCTI to begin raising consciousness about domestic violence in local communities. Eventually they sought and secured a grant from an NGO in Holland for a community intervention. Meanwhile, an L&C graduate student (Balazsy, personal communication, July 2, 2015) designed and is carrying out thesis research with faculty at BMCTI, calling on local Ugandan counseling experts to define and describe domestic violence from a local, culturally-informed perspective through focus group discussions. An adaptation of the power and control wheel is being developed through this research for use in Uganda. Faculty and staff at BMCTI have already begun using what has been adapted thus far in their work in the community.

BMCTI faculty and staff are reaching out to community leaders and local authorities to train them in recognizing signs of abuse, discussing safety issues, reporting crimes associated with abuse, understanding the cycle of abuse, and referring those in need to BMCTI, where there are resources for counseling (in part supported by It Takes a Village Uganda). Counseling experts at BMCTI have tailored their community interventions to fit their cultural context by collaborating with clan elders and religious leaders. Clan elders are most often without formal education, but their wisdom is highly respected in the community. When domestic violence occurs, they are the first to receive complaints. The cultural, traditional, and natural wisdom of these helpers has been enriched with practical knowledge of abuse cycles. They are now using this knowledge to inform their decisions on behalf of clan members. For example, if a husband beats his wife, the wife will likely go to her parents' home. Traditionally when a wife has gone to her parents, her husband has an obligation to appeal to her family and the clan elder in order to seek reconciliation. The husband is typically given a punishment and the wife returns to the marriage. Clan elders are now beginning to enter these situations with a better understanding of the abuse cycle. They are less likely to be deceived by the husband's show of remorse or promises to change. They realize that all might not be well when a couple is in a "honeymoon stage." They are slower to move toward reconciliation and more likely to say things like "you tell us now that everything is OK, but we need to go deeper into the cycle to get to the root of the problem." They are better able to recognize their own limits in solving this problem and are aware of how to refer clan members for help. Clan elders and religious leaders have significant leverage in referring families for counseling, and in helping to overcome the stigma associated with mental health issues. When sent by a clan elder or religious leader people are more likely to accept help. It is not unusual for someone to come to the counseling center at BMCTI saying, "I did not think I would come here, but my elder told me this is what I need to do" or "My clan leader told me if I don't come here, he won't listen to me again." Clan elders and religious leaders sometimes consult directly with faculty and staff at BMCTI. In this way, these informal helpers are getting consultation for their work as well as opportunities to develop their skills without pursuing a degree. They can seek support when situations get complex. They are also empowered by drawing on the expertise of the center. For example, it is not uncommon for a community leader to say, "This is what Dr. Kabura has said."

This example demonstrates the principles we outline below for collaborative humanitarianism. War, the AIDS pandemic, and economic disaster have shaken the communities in which we work. There are few material resources and high levels of stress. Traditional gender roles, supported by colonization, contribute to gendered violence. Intervening in domestic violence at the community level is a form of humanitarianism in this context. Access to published materials, resources to translate published materials into local languages, collaborative education, joint research, and funds to support this series of community interventions have been shared between funders, on the one hand, and Ugandan and Western collaborators (from, e.g., the United States and the Netherlands), on the other. While information and financial assistance from the global North has been shared with collaborators in the global South, decisions about accepting, adapting, and using the information have been made at the local level.

Guiding Principles

Working toward collaborative humanitarianism starts with placing our work in sociopolitical and historical context, as we described above. It also includes understanding humanitarianism as benefitting all of us, as deferring to local decision making, as working directly with each other, as paying attention to the outcomes of our efforts, and as caring for our relationships. Following are descriptions of the principles we apply to our work as we strive toward mutual respect and collaboration.

Acknowledging the Benefits for All From our perspective, collaborative humanitarianism turns away from the concept of humanitarianism as defined by individual internal intention, the requirement that humanitarianism must be (can be) a selfless act performed solely for an unknown other (Barnett and Weiss, p. 17). Instead, we see acts of humanitarianism as benefitting all of us within a collective. This includes clarity and openness about how engaging in humanitarian effort touches and inspires the humanity in all involved. Even reading or hearing a story of giving or doing for another inspires us to access what we typically call "our own humanity".

In the example above, collaboration between the L&C and the BMCTI faculty and students resulted in an important community intervention that will benefit the health and welfare of many Ugandans. It has also provided opportunity for the L&C group to learn about community intervention and cultural adaptation of typical counseling and psychoeducational tools used in family therapy. We share this example in classes at L&C to inspire creative systemic thinking and to encourage the tailoring of family-based community interventions in ways that are culturally and contextually situated. The L&C student who completed her thesis also had a unique opportunity to learn how to collaborate on research at a transnational level.

Prioritizing Local Decision Making Applying for outside aid typically includes fitting local needs into foreign funder agendas. NGOs determine the focus of the work through their defined areas of interest, which typically reflect the Western values and agendas of the global North. Even the process of applying, and the strategic planning that this entails, requires locals to adopt a Western framework. Funders often require local agencies to have the capacity to absorb funds, as demonstrated by large existing working budgets. While these funding streams are important and useful, we believe that humanitarianism is more collaborative when local decision making is prioritized. We assume that experts working in their own communities have the best ideas about what is most helpful, about who should be employed to do what, and about how funds can be used/stretched to make the greatest impact.

In the example above, it was important that outside "experts" did not enter the Ugandan context with a solution to be imposed locally. The decisions to mobilize against domestic violence, the language and meaning around the public education approach and materials (e.g., the version of the power and control wheel developed in Uganda), and the strategic plan to use traditional pathways for problem solving were made at the local level by the counseling experts in Uganda.

Keeping it Simple Collaborative humanitarianism encourages small, individual-to-individual acts in which funding is as direct as possible, with little or no overhead for organizational costs. Funding streams often start as rivers in the global North, but as they pass through and are diverted to outside experts on their way to those on the ground in the global South, the river becomes a trickle. Capacity-building efforts to address community mental health and relational needs can sometimes mistakenly overemphasize the role of outside expertise. This by its very nature undervalues inside expertise. For example, it is not uncommon for Westerners to feel compelled to work in Uganda once we see the high level of need in the daily lives of most Ugandans. There are specific professions in which there is a shortage (e.g., doctors, dentists) and spaces in which volunteerism is essential; however, there are also many Ugandans ready and willing to take on most roles. For a Western counselor to travel to Uganda and work with children and families for one week would not only be ethically questionable but would also cost upward of three thousand dollars. This same amount would support a qualified master's-level Ugandan counselor educator for seven or eight months.

At the broadest level of meaning we share humanitarian goals with a worldwide community of mental health professionals dedicated to promoting human welfare. Our work is, however, more specifically placed in the realm of humanitarianism relative to the idea of those with more resources providing assistance to those with fewer resources. On a practical level, U.S. partners need to assume greater financial responsibility for collaboration. We share the goal of supporting counselor training and community mental health efforts in Uganda as a humanitarian agenda that can be supported in part through financial help from the West.

It is clear in the example above that we made direct person-to-person connections, which evolved into a community intervention. Faculty at BMCTI and L&C decided together to include domestic violence in the family therapy training curriculum. They shared the experience of witnessing the significant impact this information had on course participants. The resulting enthusiasm led to collaborative research and to the use of local knowledge by BMCTI to create and seek funding for a community intervention. Financial aid was offered directly to those on the ground, who are using the funds to produce materials and pay for staff and faculty outreach. Our work through It Takes a Village Uganda mirrors this approach, as there is very little organizational overhead and nearly all funds are used directly for faculty and staff development, basic in-country organizational needs, and local community interventions in Uganda.

Paying Attention to Outcome It has been suggested that humanitarianism can only be accurately defined by its outcome (Barnett and Weiss 2008). We have seen case after case of well-intended efforts causing harm; in the examples in this paper,

Westerners delivered expert-driven trainings in northern Uganda and an NGO helped some but not all child-headed families in the Kabarole District. As noted above, both of these well-intended efforts resulted in at least some lasting negative consequences.

In our work, we use the concepts of transferability, authenticity, and confirmability from qualitative research to guide the process of sharing ideas and practices from one context to another. Transferability has to do with how what we find in one context might be true or useful in another. This requires comprehensive consideration of the similarities and differences between contexts. At times, attempts to share knowledge and practices from one setting to another are—and should be—rejected. Sometimes they are accepted; sometimes they are altered, something new emerges as in the case example above, in which counselors in Uganda used their expert knowledge about local expressions of domestic violence to develop community education tools and used these tools in ways that leveraged change through existing traditional social arrangements. Local experts reflected on what might or might not transfer to their context and on how ideas could be shaped for their local context. Including a diverse group of counselors in these discussions in Uganda added authenticity to the process. Confirmability can only be evaluated once the new idea or practice is used or tested in the new setting. While BMCTI is currently conducting program evaluation, it is already clear from the positive community response and referrals to BMCTI for help that the domestic violence community intervention is working.

Attending to Relationships It is through our relationships with each other that we experience humanitarian transformation. This is not only about the care we offer others; it is about the care we take of each other via the activity and intention of helping for the sake of the common good. Humanitarian connections require us to be accountable for using our relative positions of power to contribute to just practices, to be open in our approach to cross-cultural work, to have humility in our continuous self-reflection, and to continuously navigate and explore the value of difference in the process of maintaining our ongoing connection.

In the example above, we all grew together in our knowledge of the cultural expression of domestic violence and in our abilities to creatively intervene at a community level. We attended to our relationships with each other throughout. For us, relationships come first. This means engaging in give and take, being transparent about who is in the lead in which context and why, and governing our collaborations with an eye to what is just and fair. We would not have allowed anyone from L&C to complete research in Uganda without working alongside faculty at BMCTI to ensure correct cultural interpretation and to share professional credit for research results. We continuously negotiate how workshops are designed and how to redistribute material resources from the United States for work being done in Uganda. We strive to be kind and respectful toward each other, enjoying the good will and humor generated by our relationship. We negotiate differences with openness, keeping the interests of all in mind. We have developed deep friendships as a result.

Conclusion

The work we have done together has not been extraordinary, but the results of our work have been. Simple acts of working together toward common goals, caring for and learning from each other, setting our sights on what is best for the whole, truthfully acknowledging global inequities and finding ways to minimize their effects, and comparing and contrasting common human problems across diverse contexts have sustained our lasting and effective humanitarian efforts. Students and faculty at L&C are deepening their sense of global identity, growing in their global awareness, and working to redistribute material resources. Students and faculty at BMCTI are energized when there are opportunities for shared learning, feel hopeful when their efforts are supported, and are deeply committed to helping their communities. Engaging in humanitarian work together has helped all of us access the better parts of who we are, and has connected us to a shared humanity much greater than the sum of ourselves, our relationships, and our efforts.

References

Anzaldua, G. (2007). *Borderlands: La frontera* (3rd ed.). San Francisco, CA: Aunt Lute Books.

Barnett, M., & Weiss, T. (2008). *Humanitarianism in question: Politics, power, ethics*. Ithaca, NY: Cornell University Press.

Bourdieu, P. (1986). The forms of capital. In J. G. Richardson (Ed.), *Handbook of theory and research for the sociology of education* (pp. 241–258). New York, NY: Greenwood Press.

Hudson, C. (2012). Disparities in the geography of mental health: Implications for social work. *Social Work, 57*(2), 107–119. doi:10.1093/sw/sws001.

Kipp, W., Satzingerb, F., Alibhai, A., & Rubaale, T. (2010). Needs and support for Ugandan child-headed households: Results from qualitative study. *Vulnerable Children and Youth Studies: An International Interdisciplinary Journal for Research, Policy and Care, 5*(4), 297–309. doi:10.1080/17450128.2010.507805.

McDowell, T. (2015). *Applying critical social theory to family therapy practice*. New York, NY: Springer.

Schimmel, N. (2010). Failed aid: How development agencies are neglecting and marginalizing Rwandan genocide survivors. *Development in Practice, 20*(3), 407–413.

Thiede, B., & Brown, D. (2013). Hurricane Katrina: Who stayed and why? *Population Research and Policy Review, 32*(6), 803–824. doi:10.1007/s11113-013-9320-9.

Collaborative Therapy with Women and Children Refugees in Houston: Moving Toward Rehabilitation in the United States After Enduring the Atrocities of War

Manjushree Palit and Susan B. Levin

Support Group Work with Refugee Women and Children

The refugee group project began when a helping agency in Houston, Texas, working closely with refugee women and children, invited Houston Galveston Institute (HGI) therapists to collaborate. The supervised clinical associates of HGI are doctoral and master's-degree students in marriage and family therapy programs, and receive their clinical training in collaborative therapy under the supervision of HGI faculty. The first author, MP (a doctoral student in the Marriage and Therapy Program at Virginia Polytechnic Institute and State University, led the team of supervised clinical associates under the supervision of the second author, SL, a faculty member at HGI. The supervised clinical associates were a multicultural group of therapists) from India, Mexico, Trinidad and Tobago, and the therapeutic relationships. The diverse group of therapists included therapists who were immigrants. Similarly, the refugee women and children came from different countries in Central Africa (Burundi, Cameroon, Rwanda, the Democratic Republic of Congo, Tanzania, Uganda, and Sudan). The support group therapy sessions took place once every week for three and half hours, over a period of approximately two months. The location of our therapy work with the refugee community was a one-bedroom apartment in the apartment complex where the refugee women lived with their families in Houston. This space was provided by the helping agency. The big living

M. Palit (✉)
Jindal Institute of Behavioral Sciences, O.P. Jindal Global University, Sonipat,
NCR Delhi, India
e-mail: mpalit@jgu.edu.in

S.B. Levin
Houston Galveston Institute, Houston, TX, USA
e-mail: suetalkhgi@gmail.com

room space was filled with a huge table around which we sat. It was used for group therapy with between seven and fifteen women. The bedroom space was used for the group work with ten to fifteen teenage children.

Needs of Refugee Women and Children

The United Nations High Commissioner for Refugees (UNHCR) (2013) recommends Mental Health and Psychosocial Support (MHPSS) for persons of concern in humanitarian settings. MHPSS practitioners and academicians have criticized the "deficit" model-based approach that has been used with this population. The deficit model presumes that refugees as a group are helpless and traumatized, and that they need to focus on conversations about their experience of war and atrocities.

When working with people who have suffered from the abuse of power, greater sensitivity is needed in building a safe and trusting therapeutic relationship. Reichelt and Sveaass (1994) state that when working with refugee families, therapists should identify the refugee families' needs clearly rather than focusing on the issues that stand out for them (the therapists). Therapists' ability to initiate and receive clients' feedback can influence the success of therapy (Duncan et al. 2004).

Using Collaborative Therapy in Refugee Support Group Work

We used the collaborative therapy model in our work with refugees. While many clinicians we know would say that their work is collaborative, the theory of this model originates at HGI. Harlene Anderson and Harold (Harry) Goolishian, the founders of collaborative therapy, first called this approach collaborative language systems. Anderson first used this term in handouts for a workshop called "Therapeutic Impasses with Difficult Clients: A Collaborative Language Systems Approach." This workshop went a step beyond family systems to a language systems perspective (see Anderson and Goolishian 1988, 1992). Anderson (1990) outlines specific details about the therapist's role and stance, the therapeutic process, and elements of therapeutic conversations. In it, the not-knowing stance, creating space, mutual puzzling, and other key elements of collaborative therapy are presented. The collaborative process is characterized as a being "in-there-together." The client and therapist are described as equal partners in the creation of the diagnosis and the cure; dialogue and conversation are the avenues through which the therapist can open space for the client's meaning system to change and shift. These ideas were radical at the time they were introduced. Today, however, collaborative therapy is a well-established model of family therapy used worldwide. It also values common factors and incorporates client input beyond gathering feedback, by allowing the feedback to steer and determine the direction of therapy.

Creating a Dialogical Space

In collaborative therapy, one of the explicit roles of the therapist is that of an architect who facilitates a conversational space (Anderson and Goolishan 1988). Making your clients comfortable is essential throughout the process of therapy; working with refugees who were unaccustomed to the culture of talk therapy as it exists in the United States required us to constantly rethink how we offered services to them. One thing we did was to arrange, along with the helping agency, for food (fruits and snacks) and water during the group work. The groups were scheduled in the afternoon for three and half hours, and many children attended the group work immediately after school and were hungry at that time of the day. Sensitivity to the needs of each group member is crucial in building rapport, in beginning to bridge differences, and in facilitating a constructive environment.

In our work with a mixed population of refugee women and children from different countries in sub-Saharan Africa, we sought to hear, respectfully acknowledge, and connect with each group member in the hopes we could facilitate the dialogical space. Child care was essential during the time the mothers were in group therapy. Many group members availed themselves of this option: they could check on their children and feed them, and yet also disengage from caregiving and participate in the group therapy.

One challenge in creating dialogical conversation with this group was, literally, language. Or rather, the lack of us using the same one. Most of the refugee women and children were fluent in Swahili, and some were somewhat fluent in English and French. All therapists were fluent in English; one was also fluent in Spanish and another in south east Asian languages, but none were fluent in Swahili. A female interpreter who was fluent in Swahili was invited at the outset to facilitate communication; before the group itself started to meet she and the HGI therapists spent considerable time discussing the challenges involved. Translation informed the pace of the work: we slowed everything down.

We started the group with a simple icebreaker activity that introduced the members to the therapists and interpreter in a nonthreatening manner and required limited use of conversation. We used a ball and rolled it across the table around which everyone was seated. Whoever received the ball had a chance to share her name and favorite color by picking from among the colorful markers placed in the center of the table. In this way the women and the therapists got to know each other's names and favorite color. The second time the ball was passed around the table, each person went to the map (food and her home country).

This activity encouraged greater participation and seemed a safe invitation to share things about ourselves. Ironically, we think that this cocreated nontalking activity actually improved the dialogical space. Similarly, an icebreaker activity with the children generated a lot of laughter and dialogue (most children spoke Swahili, some spoke and understood English, and a few could speak French as well). The one available interpreter worked with the women; there were no interpreters available for the children, but children who spoke English translated for the ones who did not. This triggered conversations between the children and HGI therapists about their length of stay in the United States, their time at school, and their interests in joining school soon.

The Client Is the Expert

The client is the expert; the therapist invites the client to share expertise about situations, problems, and perspectives in the dialogical process of transformation (Anderson and Goolishian 1992). The label *collaborative* refers to the dedication to a mutual process of coevolving meaning. More than a technique, this is a philosophical stance (Anderson 2007). The therapists lay aside their preconceived notions and invite questions and curiosity. It is especially useful when working with multiple systems.

Three distinct systems informed our group therapy session: the helping agency that contracted the therapeutic work to HGI (for a fixed period), the refugee women, and the HGI therapists. Each system can have different expectations and objectives for the group session. The not-knowing stance encouraged a healthy discussion, clarity, and transparency about the (hidden) agendas from all ends. On the contrary, indirect communications and lack of disclosure about hidden agendas can generate "poor conversations" that may disrupt the therapeutic conversational practice (Reichelt and Sveaass 1994). The idea of establishing a support group for refugee women and children was conceived by the helping agency, and the purpose was to provide psychological support to address the refugee women and children's experiences of atrocities of war. The refugee women who presented themselves at the support group were curious about the purpose of the group, as they were unfamiliar with the helping agency's goals. This curiosity was explored in the contextual conversational space that ensued, and varied perspectives were shared.

Clarifying goals of the support group Therapists' response to clients and their knowledge is crucial to the development and quality of the therapeutic relationship (Anderson and Goolishian 1988). During the first group session, two staff members from the helping agency, who remained present throughout the duration of the support group, were invited to share their understanding about the group's purpose. The refugee women, too, were invited to voice their understanding about the purpose of the group, as well as the type of support essential for their well-being, and the role they envisioned for the therapists. The refugee women identified several needs: to learn English to survive in the United States, to address health concerns and understand the U.S. health systems, to invite other refugee women from their community and increase their support network, and finally, to understand American culture and how people interact in this culture.

The HGI therapists, in their turn, shared that their role was to facilitate and support the women in their purpose of feeling empowered (even if that purpose changed in the course of therapy). To maintain the therapeutic alliance it was important to understand the challenges of unexpressed (hidden) agendas, and to address them in a way that was amicable for all parties concerned. This conversation (about hidden agendas) generated information about the clients' perspectives concerning their needs, available resources, fears, and curiosity in the present. Similar views were expressed by the authors. Therefore, in keeping with this feedback the remaining sessions were designed collaboratively by the therapists and the refugee women and children.

Narratives about adjustment in the United States One group discussion, on adjustment in the United States, revealed poignant narratives about the women and children's experiences in the United States. The dialogue about language further unraveled their concerns that learning English could empower them to seek jobs, respond to people in socially acceptable ways, and facilitate their adjustment in this foreign land. They felt scared, unhappy, and limited in their adjustment and survival skills. They believed that their lack of English-language fluency prevented them from getting jobs and responding in culturally appropriate ways. The need to learn English was also emphasized in the children's support group. After this discussion we assessed resources available within and for this community—in particular, the availability of English-language courses.

Adjustment for the children was also something we learned a lot about. Children discussed the challenge of acclimatizing both to the Houston weather (much hotter and more humid than the colder climate they were used to) and to the school system. Many children shared that they had difficulty being comfortable with other students; they felt safe with friends in their community and therefore interacted with them only. Language was a big barrier! Yet those who did understand U.S. English struggled in other subjects like algebra and geography. Conversations about the climate, schooling, and living conditions revealed new information about the homeland, as well. Most children in the group shared that they preferred the refugee camps to their homes or farms, as they had had at least two meals a day as opposed to barely one.

Engaging in dialogue about expectations and reality about life in United States The group was encouraged by the therapists to share about their impression of America and whether it was different from what they had heard. This question encouraged discussion about the divide between expectations and ground reality. It generated information about each one's length of stay in United States; challenges in seeking jobs; issues navigating social settings (bus stops, train stations, hospitals, and church and school situations); and difficulties experienced in communicating with people from other communities in the United States. The women in the group were curious to understand American culture and how to interact and fit in. Their understanding of body language helped them a little socially. They shared their experiences and we shared a few of ours. For example, one therapist from India shared that access to specialist health care practitioners is different in the United

States than in her home country. In the following group therapy session, suggestions were invited from members who had stayed here longer, on ways to navigate life here. The group generated useful information, resources, and how to overcome fears in this new world.

Another important need expressed by the refugee women concerned health care. It became apparent that they failed to understand the procedures and were petrified of accessing the health care system. They shared about the facilities and services they had received upon arrival in this country, including shelter, food, Medicaid (health insurance), schooling for their children, and food stamps. Burnett and Peel (2001) have said that refugees who come from countries where the health care system is not well developed have different expectations; for example of being referred to the hospital system for illnesses that, here, can usually be treated in primary care settings. This can frustrate and disappoint refugees who are unfamiliar with the health care system of developed nations. Therefore, access to medication should be made simple for this population: their experiences and unmet expectations can shape their adjustment and development of coping mechanisms in this foreign land (Burnett and Peel 2001). The HGI therapists collaborated with the helping agency and with experts (English teaching, medical professionals, and members from the refugee community who had successfully transitioned to the United States) to address the group's needs.

Strategies addressing the support group's needs Burnett and Peel (2001) said that refugees and asylum seekers have manifold needs: physical, psychological, community engagement and counseling over an extended period of time. The helping agency arranged for the English course to be resumed in the same apartment complex. A session was planned and arranged with a guest speaker, a pediatrician from the medical community who addressed health care needs regarding nutrition and immunizations.

Most women in this group had young children or were caring for children, hence they highly appreciated the pediatrician speaking with them. Cleanliness and personal hygiene were also addressed in this community. Further information regarding access to medical care, such as which area doctors accepted Medicaid and administered HPV immunizations were provided as requested by the group. The helping agency decided to intermittently set up talks by speakers from the medical professions to improve the community's understanding of the health care system in United States.

Further, another "advice" session was arranged with a young woman and her mother from the refugee community, who had immigrated to the United States long ago. The young woman was educated and currently holding a job here and so was her mother. This family had successfully transitioned to their life in the United States. Such a talk helped both the women and children understand the tools, nuances, and tips to navigate the foreign culture, education, health care and community from a member of their community. The above facilitated further discussion and participation from more members of the refugee community.

Having facilitated a discussion about needs and usefulness of the support group, it was important to discuss about the limitations and duration of the support group. Is it possible to meet all the needs through the support group within two months? If not, how else could they be met for this community? Therapists informed the refugee women and children about the duration and limitations of the support group, and incorporated a small change in the future groups.

Every session henceforth, the therapists spent 15 min teaching and addressing questions that the group members had about the American table manners, greetings and responses to greetings. Coaching, although not regularly used unless needed in therapy, was used with this particular population. Learning and practicing how to introduce one's self was a requested and important skill.

Feedback using the mutually agreed upon common sign language (showing one thumb signifying "good job" and two thumbs "a very good job") helped improve the coaching and learning experience. Being open, flexible, responsive and present with the client are core components of collaborative therapy and crucial for therapeutic alliance. This encouraged trust, discussion and empowered the group members to exchange learning. They taught us how to greet in Swahili, a language with which the therapists were unfamiliar and we taught them a few words of English. Finally, the helping agency affirmed that English classes will resume and regular talks from health professionals will be scheduled for this community.

The Not-Knowing Stance

"Knowledge is an interactive process in which all parties contribute and what is created is unique and has relevancy and usefulness for that community of persons" (Anderson 2007). Using the not-knowing stance, the HGI therapists refrained from making assumptions based on outside or non-local knowledge and treating all refugee women from the African continent as a homogenous group with one defining experience and invited their voices in identifying and addressing their needs. Through exercises in sentence building in English, the refugee women discussed levels of stress, mental health issues, and their coping mechanisms from stressors. Finally, in the natural course of the shared dialogue and knowledge creation between the therapists' and clients', mental health, psychosocial support, coping mechanism were discussed and transformation was experienced.

Not-knowing what it means to be a woman or child in this community A collage activity was introduced to create a conversational space and leave room for the conversation that one chose, if one chose to do so. Each participant had the choice to bring what they wanted to bring into the conversation or refrain from what they did not. The activity was to create a collage of what it means to be a woman. Therapists provided magazines for creating collages. The refugee women in the group were instructed that they could rip out any picture from the magazines and stick them on the white sheet of collage paper with a glue stick. Once they felt they were done with the collage they could stop, if not they continued till they felt the collage was complete. Conversational space created through this activity generated a lot of interest and discussion. The group members were informed that if they did not want to participate, they need not do so. The women selected several pictures and shared several gender narratives—a woman should keep herself beautiful, healthy and clean, physically and mentally healthy for the family's well-being and is considered responsible for others (husband and the children).

Not-knowing and the pre and post displacement narratives Post displacement narratives revealed that women felt powerless with their children. Children learnt English quickly and were the translators for the family and powerful in social settings in American culture. Therefore, mothers struggled with disciplining and imposing authority on their children in this country. Pre displacement narratives shared were horrifying stories of trauma, abuse, missing family members, family members left behind, hopelessness and helplessness of having their family scattered. For example, one particular story was of two sisters, one silent and one more talkative in the session. During the support group session, the silent sister started sobbing and the talkative one told their story of horror. Their teenage brother was burnt alive by attackers' right outside the home of the silent sister. Desperately she tried to save him and in the process burnt both her hands. Unfortunately she couldn't save her brother because he had suffered third degree burns. Another story shared was of a mother who ran away with her daughter to save her from being abducted and gang raped. Unfortunately, in the attempt to run away, her husband was left behind but she reached safely with her daughter to United States. Many stories shared were of women being abducted, raped by men with guns, lost children, lack of freedom to raise voices against atrocities, disruption of livelihood, and being fearful for their and lives of loved ones.

The stories revealed that some women were experiencing depression, anxiety, were having difficulty getting out of bed and doing their daily chores, experiencing body pain, having sleeping difficulties, and feeling less energetic or enthusiastic about life here. In the children's group, a similar activity focused on the topic of what it means to be a child. Their narratives had similar stories of abuse, trauma, life in refugee camps or farms, running for their lives, moving periodically, of lost family members, and fears. Many shared narratives of being afraid and being bullied and discriminated as a racial group in the United States. They shared present stories of being harassed by other children because of their skin color. They also shared hopes of being accepted, managing relationships and having a better life in the United States. They further shared stories of being the translator for families, or helping parents understand the system and navigate the American way of life. We thanked the women and children for sharing their stories and this activity was conducted separately for both groups.

Resilience, Coping and Support System

Being present with the group allowed us to be tentative and flexible to the conversation that ensued about people's narratives and focus on the psychosocial support, resources, and resilience amongst the community members. The group of refugee women and children shared their narratives at their own pace. It gave us an insight into what it means to be a woman or a child from their community. Further, this discussion guided the therapists' to direct the course of the remaining sessions in exploring coping and support system. Women and children supported each other with words and gestures when someone from the group was in tears. The community played a key role in staying in touch with their homeland, their culture, shared stories, mental health, in their healing and adjustment in this foreign land. A dialogue not only encourages sharing of one's personal stories but also presents an opportunity to expand and elaborate on the newness (Anderson and Levin 1998). Keeping in mind, "witness" or "being present with the client", the HGI therapists encouraged conversation about how the women and children defined their support system and choose to support each other's adjustment here.

Coping with trauma Therefore, instead of presuming the right coping mechanisms for community, the therapists using the not-knowing stance invited the group members to expand on their existing resources or develop new resources to help the community cope with trauma and stressors. The group focused on methods or means that can help the women and children cope with the pain and trauma and give them hope and peace. The group identified community gatherings where they played their music and cooked their traditional foods (different from American foods) helped them bond and prevent isolation. Affiliation to a Church or religious community helped them connect with others and prevent further isolation of the community. Burnett and Peel (2001) have emphasized that refugees' experience isolation and disengagement and that affiliation to religious organizations can prevent isolation and help them cope with the loss and trauma. By listing their own resources, both human and material, the group was able to enhance their capacity for self-help and social support that contribute to good health.

In conversation regarding coping with trauma and stressors, new techniques were introduced by the HGI therapists such as Mandalas and progressive relaxation techniques with the group. These self-soothing techniques were discussed to help cope with the recurrent intrusive thoughts that disturbed sleep, or when the women felt stressed or anxious. Feedback was gathered from the group about the usefulness of both the Mandalas and self-soothing exercises. Mandala exercises have been known to have similar effects as meditation (Curry and Kasser 2005). They received the most positive feedback from the group as compared to the progressive relaxation techniques. Therefore, each woman in the support group received their take-home packet of mandala prints and color pencil sets.

Coping with loss, planning remembrance and concluding session collaboratively The purpose of this discussion was to address the survivor's feelings of guilt and loss. A joint session with both refugee women and children focused on identifying culturally appropriate methods of coping and commemorating the dead or lost or left behind members of their family. Abrupt and unnecessary loss of life, chaos and conflict were the predominant narratives of this community. Therefore, planning and creating a ritual suggested by the group (such as celebrating or assigning a day for remembering the loved ones who were lost or left behind) presented an experiential opportunity to practice a new narrative of addressing survivors' guilt. The refugee women and children came up with two options. Some decided that they would like to color the mandalas and create a "mandala collage" in memory of their loved ones who are either lost or left behind or deceased. Others decided to create bracelets with the names of their lost family members; symbolizing their way of honoring and remembering their loved ones. The brainstorming session empowered the refugee women and children to choose a way to commemorate and conclude the last support group session with the HGI therapists. In addition, the women and especially the teenagers made a special request to commemorate the therapeutic collaboration—HGI therapists could teach them a song in English and in turn they teach the HGI therapists a song in Swahili.

Consequently, in the final session, an atmosphere of celebration and remembrance was created and included food, celebratory decorations, quotes in English and Swahili. Some women and children colored the mandalas and created a community mandala collage and others created bracelets in the session and wore it around their wrist as a mark of remembrance. This ritual facilitated expression of deeper emotions and the women and children were invited to share a few words in memory of the loved one (if they were willing and comfortable doing the same). The symbolic meaning associated with the ritual was to represent the good in their life, to have faith, hope, and peace. Finally the session ended with teenagers singing one song in Swahili and another in French, and the HGI therapists sang a song in English reciprocating and respecting the support group's request to commemorate the last session. This ritual was significant for the support group women and children and was a special way of thanking each other and the HGI therapists joined in this shared dialogical ritual of collaborative thankfulness.

Conclusion

Collaborative therapy emphasizes the idea of "walking with the client"; recognizing the client's need, pace, expertise in situational context and creating safe dialogical space (Anderson 2007). The not-knowing stance of the therapists' is open for challenge and change in the therapeutic process (Anderson and Levin 1998). In keeping with the philosophical understandings of Collaborative Therapy, the methodology we used in the support group work was—be flexible, "be present with the group", and develop an equal and collaborative partnership from the beginning till the termination of the group. We valued the therapeutic alliance and feedback throughout the course of therapy. Common factor researchers, Duncan et al. (2004) emphasized the need to include clients' voices in treatment to increase outcome effectiveness. UNHCR (2013) emphasized the need for resilience and resource focused approach in humanitarian settings to empower persons of concerns (POC) and facilitate their adjustment post displacement based on consistent research findings. HGI therapists and clients formed a collaborative dialogical engagement, and listened to the support groups' voice in directing the course of the brief group therapy and maximizing the outcome effectiveness for the refugee women and children.

The strength of Collaborative Therapy model is that it encourages therapists' to be flexible, sensitive to the voices of POC, and freedom to be curious and explore the existing resources, community support and resilience present in the refugee community as underlined by UNHCR report (2013). Finally, we would like to point out that we do not believe that Collaborative Therapy is a final product and is the best way to do therapy. We value life-long learning and our ongoing experiences and relationships with colleagues, clients and others in the field of mental health, among others, influence our work and our ideas. Harry Goolishian was known to say that if his ideas had not changed 10 % each year he was not working hard enough.

Acknowledgement The collaborative support group work with refugee women and children was possible because of the contributions of the HGI therapists—Andres Romero, Debra Wells, Josie Paul, Megan Harris, and Manjushree Palit (author). This team of HGI therapists was clinically supervised by Dr. Susan Levin (coauthor). Finally, a vote of thanks to Houston Galveston Institute for its diverse, extensive, and supportive clinical training program.

References

Anderson, H. (1990). *Therapeutic impasses with difficult clients: A collaborative language systems approach* (Unpublished).

Anderson, H. (2007). *The therapist and the postmodern therapy system: A way of being with others*. Retrieved from http://www.europeanfamilytherapy.eu/wp-content/uploads/2012/10/anderson.pdf

Anderson, H., & Goolishian, H. (1988). Human systems as linguistic systems: Evolving ideas about the implications for theory and practice. *Family Process, 27*, 371–393.

Anderson, H., & Goolishian, H. (1992). The client is the expert: A not-knowing approach to therapy. In S. McNamee & K. Gergen (Eds.), *Therapy as social construction* (pp. 25–39). Newbury Park, CA: Sage.

Anderson, H., & Levin, S. B. (1998). Generative conversations: A postmodern approach to conceptualizing and working with human systems. In M. F. Hoyt (Ed.), *The handbook of constructive therapies: Innovative approaches from leading practitioners* (pp. 46–67). San Francisco, CA: Jossey-Bass.

Burnett, A., & Peel, M. (2001). Asylum seekers and refugees in Britain: Health needs of asylum seekers and refugees. *British Medical Journal, 322*, 544–547.

Curry, N. A., & Kasser, T. (2005). Can coloring mandalas reduce anxiety? *Art Therapy: Journal of the American Art Therapy Association, 22*, 81–85.

Duncan, B. L., Miller, S. D., & Sparks, J. (2004). *The heroic client: A revolutionary way to improve effectiveness through client-directed, outcome-informed therapy*. San Francisco, CA: Jossey-Bass.

Reichelt, S., & Sveaass, N. (1994). Therapy with refugee families: What is a "good" conversation? *Family Process, 33*, 247–262.

United Nations High Commissioner for Refugees. (2013). *UNHCR's mental health and psychosocial support for persons of concern*. Retrieved from http://www.unhcr.org/51bec3359.pdf

Ofreciendo Terapia En El Idioma De Preferencia Del Cliente: El Modelo De Preparación Profesional Calificada En Dos Idiomas De Ollu

Joan L. Biever and Jeanette Santos

Introduction

> I really enjoyed your class [Lifespan Development], though when I was home over Christmas break, I didn't have the language to explain what I learned to my friends who are mothers.

This reflection was from a student from Mexico City after my (JLB) first semester of teaching at Our Lady of the Lake University (OLLU). As a monolingual English speaker, I was puzzled by this statement. I had no way of understanding why someone who was a native Spanish speaker was unable to translate what she had learned in English to Spanish. As I discussed this dilemma with colleagues, we became aware of the complexity of applying what is learned in one language to working in a second language. Abstract ideas and concepts are difficult to translate linguistically and culturally. For example, the use of metaphors and "dichos" (proverbs) are difficult to translate and understand because they are culturally based and the meaning not always comparable in both languages, even when literally translated. Another example is the use of everyday or colloquial words such as "collaboratively" (when trying to get every member of the family involved). The translation "en colaboracion" does not capture the depth of "equally working together toward a goal" instead in Spanish it means "some help"; these language nuances are difficult to translate with the mere help of dictionary. In addition, other constructs derived from theoretical approaches are difficult to the practice in Spanish, for example the meaning of "the self" is not easily translated into Spanish as the construct of "the self" does not exist in many Latino cultures.

Providing Therapy in the Client's Preferred Language: The Ollu Model for Professional Competence in Two Languages.

J.L. Biever (✉) · J. Santos
Our Lady of the Lake University, San Antonio, TX, USA
e-mail: jbiever@ollusa.edu

© American Family Therapy Academy 2016
L.L. Charlés and G. Samarasinghe (eds.), *Family Therapy in Global Humanitarian Contexts*, AFTA SpringerBriefs in Family Therapy,
DOI 10.1007/978-3-319-39271-4_5

These discussions eventually lead to the development of the Psychological Services for Spanish Speaking Populations (PSSSP) program as an option in the graduate programs in psychology and marriage and family therapy at Our Lady of the Lake University (OLLU). Both authors are affiliated with OLLU, which is a small Catholic university located in a predominantly Hispanic, low-income area of San Antonio, Texas. As department chair, Joan led the effort to develop the PSSSP program. She has researched the experiences and needs of therapists and supervisors who provide services in Spanish. Jeanette started the doctoral program in counseling psychology in 2013. Jeanette, a native speaker of Spanish from Venezuela, has completed the requirements for the PSSSP certificate. She now supervises master's students providing services in Spanish at our training clinic. Jeanette has observed that it is especially challenging to conduct sessions where/when all members of the family have different levels of proficiency in both languages (English/Spanish) and the therapist is required to use both languages in session to attend to each individual's linguistic preference. We will first review the literature that addresses the challenges of, and the need for providing services in the language of the client. We will then describe the development, current status, and outcomes of the PSSSP PROGRAM.

Bilingualism and Therapy

When both the therapists and clients speak the same two (or more) languages, the choice of language in therapy can be important in the therapeutic process. Therapists may be more comfortable and confident working in the language of their training (Castaño et al. 2007; Verdinelli and Biever 2009a, b), while clients may prefer another language, most often their first language. Therapists may alter psychotherapy sessions when they interview clients in their non-dominant language by restricting what clients are able to say and limiting the recall and interpretation of events. Aguirre (2004) observed that her Spanish dominant clients were more comfortable and expressive in Spanish and that there was a "difference in the way people understand things when you can explain process to them in their own dominant language" (p. 13). Similarly, Santiago-Rivera et al. (2009) concluded clients' presentations, expressions of emotion, and behaviors differed in each language.

Emotion and memory Emotions may be experienced differently in each language spoken by people who speak more than one language (Santiago-Rivera and Altarriba 2002). Bilingual individuals have more emotional resonances in their native language. For example activities such as swearing, praying, and lying are associated with different feelings when spoken in the native language. One exception may be for children of immigrants who become more proficient in the dominant language of the new country (Caldwell-Harris 2014). Memories of experiences are stronger when people are interviewed in the language in which the experiences occurred (Marian and Neisser 2000; Schrauf and Rubin 2000). Even when there is equal proficiency in two languages, the memory's emotional texture and complexity will be stronger when the language of encoding and recall are the same (Tehrani and Vaughan 2009).

Language switching Switching languages over the course of therapy is common when the therapists and clients speak the same languages. Language switching is a valuable therapeutic tool (Santiago-Rivera et al. 2009), though many bilingual psychotherapists are concerned about how best to use this tool in a professional context (Castaño et al. 2007; Verdinelli and Biever 2009a). Santiago-Rivera et al. (2009) found that bilingual therapists used language switching to facilitate the development of a therapeutic alliance and improve effectiveness of the therapeutic process.

Bilingual/Multilingual Families

Much of the literature about bilinguals in psychotherapy considers only individual therapy (Ali 2004; Softas-Nall et al. 2015). Ali (2004) highlighted the increased complexity of family therapy when family members speak more than one language, and may have different competency levels in each language. Softas-Nall et al. (2015) emphasized the importance of exploring each family member's history of language acquisition, the patterns of current language use, and meanings associated with the use of each language. They cautioned that language usage may be associated with power issues and therefore therapists should never rely on children to translate for their parents.

Cultural and Linguistic Competence

Conducting therapy in a language other than the language of training is complex and challenging for many therapists as it requires a high level of proficiency in the language as well as cultural knowledge and understanding. Cultural and linguistic competencies are separate, but interrelated and equally important, when working with bilingual clients (Biever et al. 2002; Biever et al. 2011; Schwartz et al. 2010). Schwartz et al. (2010) noted that cultural competence included awareness of one's own and the clients' worldviews and appropriate intervention strategies. Linguistic competence was defined as "ability to communicate effectively via grammatical, conversational, sociolinguistic, and strategic accuracy and flexibility" (Schwartz et al. 2010, p. 2011).

Mere conversational proficiency in a language is not sufficient for competent mental health services in that language (Castaño et al. 2007; Biever et al. 2011; Schwartz et al. 2010; Verdinelli and Biever 2009b). Bilingual individuals differ in their relative proficiency in each language across contexts depending on how and when each language was learned (Guttfreund 1990; Valdés and Figueroa 1994) and the contexts wherein the language is maintained. English-Spanish bilingual therapists trained in English reported that that they felt less confident and competent when working in Spanish (Verdinelli and Biever 2009b). Other concerns of therapists who were trained in English but offered services in Spanish included having a limited technical vocabulary and poor ability to express psychological concepts (Castaño et al. 2007; Verdinelli and Biever 2009a, b). Bilingual therapists reported difficulty conceptualizing in Spanish, translating their thoughts from English to Spanish, and finding specific words, which resulted in delayed responses to clients and interrupted the conversational flow (Aguirre 2004; Castaño et al. 2007; Verdinelli and Biever 2009a, b, 2013). Bilingual therapists are not always aware of differences in the use of words and idioms among persons from different Spanish speaking countries and regions, which can lead to misunderstandings and uncomfortable moments (Castaño et al. 2007; Verdinelli and Biever 2009a, b, 2013). Aguirre (2004), a heritage Spanish speaker, who received her training in English, described her experiences doing family therapy in Spanish as:

> I feel inadequate because I sometimes do not have all of the right words and expressions readily available when I do therapy in Spanish. You see, although I am bilingual, I know that my capabilities in Spanish vocabulary are very much lacking. I learned the therapeutic language in English, but I do not readily have those same words and phrases in Spanish (pp. 9–10).

The Ollu Psssp Program

The OLLU psychology department offers master's degrees in Family, Couple and Individual Counseling (FCIP) and School Psychology and a Doctor of Psychology (PsyD) in Counseling Psychology. The FCIP and PsyD programs emphasize strengths-based relational approaches. Practicum training at the department's clinic, the Community Counseling Service (CCS), uses a live supervision training model with therapy teams consisting of a supervisor and 4–6 students. The CCS serves low-income, predominantly Hispanic families. We began offering Spanish language therapy teams at CCS in the 1980s. The CCS delivered needed services to our community, but did not fully meet the training needs of our students. The PSSSP program was developed in 1997 with the goal of graduating students who were equally competent in English and Spanish psychotherapy services. Ours was the first graduate program in the United States designed to train mental health professionals in two languages. The lack of attention to training bilingual practitioners before then may have been the result of the implicit, yet faulty, assumption that therapists who had developed conversational proficiency in a second language could easily transfer professional skills and knowledge obtained in the training language to work in the new language. Our academic, clinical, and supervisory experiences, however, contradicted this assumption. The PSSSP program focuses on three interrelated areas: language proficiency, cultural awareness and knowledge, and competent and sensitive service delivery in Spanish.

Development of the Psssp Program

The majority of the bilingual students in OLLU's graduate programs acquired Spanish as a first or second language in their homes. These heritage speakers, regardless of conversational fluency, did not have the language skills training needed to conduct professional conversations. When we asked students about working in Spanish during practica, heritage speakers reported difficulty in translating recently acquired knowledge to Spanish; they found themselves spending time in sessions translating those ideas from English to Spanish. All students, even those who immigrated to the United States from Spanish-speaking countries, mentioned not feeling as confident or competent working in Spanish as they were in English. This finding was consistent with the work of early bilingual educators, such as Cummins (1984), who argued that proficiency at the conversational level in a language did not guarantee that cognitively complex tasks could be conducted in that language; academic learning and professional skills do not automatically transfer from one language to another. Of even greater concern to our faculty were the students who did not take advantage of the training in Spanish available to them as students because they reported a lack of confidence in their Spanish proficiency. Ironically, they later found themselves in positions where they were the only professional in the agency who spoke Spanish. Consequently, they were required to provide services in Spanish without even the supervision of a bilingual professional. They then faced the ethical dilemma of either furnishing services for which they were not fully competent or denying those services to underserved clients.

Our first step in developing the program was to hire a visiting professor from Mexico to supervise a Spanish language team at CCS and to consult with us about the development of a training program to prepare our students to meet the increasing demand for mental health services in Spanish. We then conducted surveys of bilingual psychologists in the San Antonio, Texas region to obtain their input on the need for training. None of the respondents believed they had received sufficient graduate training to provide Spanish services, especially in psychological assessment. Each professional had sought additional training, such as language classes, consultation with other Spanish-speaking professionals, and interaction with mental health professionals from México or other Spanish-speaking countries.

The respondents overwhelmingly emphasized the need for obtaining formal professional training in Spanish. Our next step was to survey 18 students who had spent at least one semester of practicum at a site that served Spanish-speaking clients. Ten rated themselves as expert and eight rated themselves as intermediate in Spanish language skills. Even those students who rated themselves as expert in reading, writing, and conversation skills in Spanish expressed concerns about the limits of their vocabularies when discussing psychological issues, theories, and interventions. These students emphasized the need for training in professional and technical Spanish and for opportunities to practice interviews and interventions before seeing Spanish-speaking clients.

The PSSSP curriculum was developed from the (a) the consultant's recommendations, (b) faculty members' observations of and experiences with training bilingual students; (c) comments and concerns expressed by bilingual students, alumni, and supervisors; (d) the recommendations of the survey respondents, and (e) review of the available literature. The program has evolved over the years as we assessed students' progress through the program. For instance, we originally had one course that focused on professional communication in Spanish but found that it became unnecessary because we began to incorporate writing and speaking in the other PSSSP courses. More recently, we added a bilingual section of the required pre-practicum course to better prepare FCIP students to offer services in Spanish in their first semester of practicum. We also varied the PSSSP requirements to better fit within the different psychology programs. The requirements for school psychology students include two courses that focus on interviews and assessment while the FCIP required courses emphasize cultural influence and social justice issues. The courses included in the PSSSP program are described below.

Curriculum

Professional/Technical Spanish was designed to improve Spanish language proficiency in work-related contexts. In-course activities allow students to contextualize grammar and vocabulary while performing language functions, such as description of processes and procedures, narration in major time frames, stating and supporting opinions, hypothesizing and counseling. Learning objectives included being able to: (a) conduct client interviews in Spanish, e.g., ask appropriate questions, make recommendations, give advice, provide instructions; (b) use advanced level grammar and concrete and abstract vocabulary in job-related language contexts, during role-plays and discussions of their clinical work, and professional articles written in Spanish; (c) understand and use technical vocabulary, sayings (*dichos*), and regional differences in meanings of words, phrases, and concepts commonly encountered during the delivery of mental health services; and (d) demonstrate Spanish language writing skills in reports and other written assignments. Students who have Spanish proficiency equivalent to a native speaker are exempted from this course; it is required for all other students.

Family Processes across Cultures is taught in English and required for all master's students. It provides familiarization with social systems on a variety of levels across diverse cultures. Learning outcomes include increasing students' awareness of their own cultural values and attitudes, their understanding of the influence of culture on therapeutic process, and competencies for working with culturally diverse clients.

Pre-practicum Counseling Laboratory (bilingual section), required for FCIP students, builds on the language skills acquired in *Professional/Technical Spanish* as students develop competency in delivering strengths-based relational therapy in both.

Language and Psychosocial Variables in Interviews and Assessments with Latinas/os is required for School Psychology students and is taught in Spanish. This course focuses on the ethnically sensitive practice and delivery of psychological assessment services to Latinas/os. Students examine the variables that influence the delivery of services to Latinas/os and how to facilitate overcoming barriers to service delivery while also improving the oral and written professional communication in Spanish.

Bilingual Assessment, taken by School Psychology and PsyD students, examines the administration and interpretation of the most frequently used psychological assessment instruments used to evaluations Spanish-speaking individuals. This course is taught bilingually.

Psychosocial Acompañamiento [Support] at the Borderlands, taken by students in the FCIP and PsyD programs, is taught in Spanish and examines responses of care to address human problems endured by Latin American communities living in the U.S. at the borderlands of political, cultural, social, historical, economic, linguistic, and institutional power.

Sociocultural Foundations of Counseling Latinas/os, which is taught in Mexico over a one to two week period, is the recommended option for FCIP and PsyD students. Students learn about the history, cultures, and mental health services delivery systems of Mexico while becoming more aware of their own cultural values. A significant experience for them is experiencing being in a language minority through the immersion experience.

Counseling Spanish Speaking Immigrants and Refugees was developed as an option for FCIP and PsyD students who were unable to take the immersion course. This course examines immigration history, policy and mental health service delivery and provides local experience in the cultures and language of Spanish speaking immigrants and refugees through field trips and local experts.

Spanish language practica are an integral component of the PSSSP program. Students spend a minimum of 8 h per week at a bilingual practicum site for three consecutive semesters. The primary site for Spanish practica is the CCS. These teams focus on the use of Spanish in conjunction with extensive discussions of theory and practice in Spanish.

Interviews with Psssp Graduates

In May 2015 we attempted to contact, by email or social media messaging, each of the fifty PSSSP program graduates. We were able to schedule interviews with 21 of the 26 graduates who responded to our initial messages. We conducted phone interviews with twenty women and one man who graduated from either the PsyD (5) or FCIP (16) programs and received their PSSSP certificate between 2002 and 2014. The participants represented every year except 2005. Eight of the 16 master's students had, or were, continuing their education in the PsyD program. Each participant selected a pseudonym used in describing our findings below.

The participants were asked to rate their confidence and competence on 10-point scale when providing services in each language. Ten indicated slightly more competence in English, while four reported equal competence in both languages, and seven rated themselves more competent in Spanish. Regardless of these differences, all participants reported that they were very competent in both languages. With respect to confidence, eleven reported more confidence in English, four reported more confidence in Spanish, and six reported equal confidence in both languages. The reported differences ranged from 1 to 2 points, indicating the self-perceived differences in competence and confidence were very low. Twenty of the 21 participants reported they were very prepared to deliver services in both languages after completing the PSSSP program.

We asked the participants (a) to describe the impact of the PSSSP program on their professional and personal development and their work with Spanish Speaking as well as non-Latino clients, (b) which components of the program were most and least helpful, (c) to describe differences they noticed between PSSSP graduates and others who provide services in Spanish, and (d) for suggestions to improve the program. Themes represented in transcripts of the interviews are discussed below.

Cultural competency Cultural competence was the most frequently occurring theme. The participants described the long-lasting effects of the PSSSP program as helping them become more curious, open-minded about, and respectful of, cultural differences. They also became more aware of their own biases. Learning about the Latino cultures, immigration history, and discrimination issues from a social justice perspective helped them embrace their own cultural identities and appreciate the diversity within and between Latino cultures, and helped them become more understanding, compassionate and better therapists. This was eloquently illustrated by two of the graduates:

> Catalina: I think it made me more compassionate and more humble… my perspective now is to interact with clients from a perspective of cultural humility in which I try to stay away of stereotyping or from my own bias and I think I'm a better therapist because of that.

> Samantha: The ability to look at things you know, power differential within language, within culture, talking about the history, talking about our experiences as bilingual immigrants, I think that made so aware of a lot of social justice issues that I wasn't very aware.

The immersion course was cited by participants as the aspect of the PSSSP program that most increased awareness of their own identity. For example, Caitlin reported that the immersion course:

> … helped me be more in touch with my heritage, my background. Really immersing yourself in the culture professionally and having that experience really helped me grow personally. I guess in the sense that allowed me to immerse two identities into one. I felt that before it was very binary (black and white) and it made me feel more comfortable immersing those two, American and Mexican identities.

Participants credited the *Professional/Technical Spanish* course and the Spanish teams as helping them appreciate the many variations of Spanish and the complexity of working with bilingual families. As Juliana stated "I think it gave me on various levels the ability to work with different people, and get to know the Spanish across the different spectrums." Bonita reported that "Especially with bilingual clients, I always ask them what is their language of preference, what is their language of emotion, their language of praying and like that."

Spanish proficiency Improving proficiency was a common theme among the participants. Bonita summarized her experience by saying: "Knowing the language, speaking the language, applying multicultural competencies and the counseling/therapeutic skills has empowered me to help those students that most need the help. These are the rewards!" Some of the participants found the program most helpful and effective in teaching them grammatically correct Spanish. The training helped develop professional terminology and overall Spanish proficiency. Maria reported, "Spanish is my first language but it was my social language, so academically I wasn't the best writer in Spanish, but she [Spanish instructor] helped me develop all of my writing skills in Spanish, as well." The participants agreed that working on the Spanish teams with live supervision facilitated their learning about using clients' language and idioms to conduct therapy, and increased their Spanish therapeutic vocabulary. These teams provided the supportive context and opportunities to overcome their reluctance about conducting therapy in Spanish and to practice their Spanish.

> Britany: … the willingness to push past the fear of saying something wrong or being embarrassed…knowing that the people that would help me with the training, the people that I was working with, weren't going to make fun of me.

> Melissa: I was a hesitant to get in the PSSSP because I thought my Spanish was very rusty, and then I got in the program and I think it helped me feel more comfortable speaking Spanish and also feel competent being able to do therapy in Spanish.

The participants identified several other benefits including: improved proficiency in Spanish, the ability to use psychological terms to communicate with other mental health professionals in Spanish, and networking with Spanish-speaking professionals in the United States and other countries.

General competence Some participants' responses described unanticipated benefits beyond increasing cultural competence and language proficiency. Several found the program and certain courses "eye-opening." Samantha stated "I think the program just made me open up my eyes to those things that I wasn't really aware of even when I started the program." Participants spoke of different ways the program increased their confidence and competence as therapists, that resulted in readiness to provide services in both English and Spanish. Jordan summarized her experience stating.

> I always think that having experiences from different cultures certainly opens your mind a lot of different things. I think has been very helpful for me. I feel like I'm more competent, so that has made me feel more confident as a professional and just personally, that has made me more competent in general no matter who comes in my office.

Participants appreciated the opportunities for self-reflection and deep exploration of their values and knowledge about the profession. For example, Janet said: "I think it help me to be more introspective and to be aware my own limitations and to assess that for myself."

Participants who completed the doctoral program recalled that experience co-supervising a Spanish team allowed them to develop supervision skills to help train other professionals to offer high quality services. According to Dee:

> Now that I am a supervisor, I am able to help the interns who are practicing now with Spanish speaking population. And we are able to do our supervision in Spanish which I think is helpful for them to continue to develop their skills.

Training differences Participants were asked to describe any differences they might have noticed with other therapists they had encountered outside of OLLU who serve Spanish-speaking clients, but had not been specifically trained to work with those populations. They all identified differences related to cultural competence and Spanish proficiency.

> Jordan: When I do therapy in Spanish I use the proper concepts and terms and know that there is a difference as I'm trying to deliver my intervention. When I've been around other people who don't have the training, I know that they're very competent in English but it does not translate in Spanish.

> Caitlin: I think it is not just having the ability to provide services in Spanish, it is knowing what you know and what you don't know about the culture of the individual. Having that open mentality and asking question, not assuming that you know them because of this. I think that is what it really comes down to the difference between the bilingual multicultural therapist and one that is not.

Challenges and Recommendations

The development of a program to train students in two languages requires faculty who are professionally proficient in both languages, training materials in the second language, sufficient numbers of bilingual students and families in the community who require services in a second language. We have been challenged to find faculty qualified to teach in Spanish, even though we are located in an area that has many professionals who identify as bilingual. We have aggressively recruited Spanish speaking faculty and provided additional support as needed. We recommend that language skills of faculty who are not native speakers who were educated in the second language should be assessed prior to teaching or supervising in that language Faculty should be supported in improving both their oral and written proficiency.

As students enter the program with a wide range of language proficiency, their proficiency in the second language should be assessed and monitored throughout the program. Having students and faculty with family origins from various Latino nations and different regions of the United States facilitates understanding of regional variations in the Spanish Language. Balancing the needs of students with varied language skills and cultural backgrounds is challenging for instructors and supervisors. Students with lower levels of proficiency may experience more stress and require additional support as they work to develop both professional and linguistic skills. Supervision of services provided in a second language should be in that language and address the complexity of language use among members of the family in the context of immigration issues, cultural beliefs and practices.

The PSSSP program is expensive for both the University and students. The University has supported the program by allowing the PSSSP courses to have smaller enrollment numbers and funding additional training for faculty to assist in their development of language skills. Finding faculty with Spanish proficiency in addition to other needed experience has required lengthier search processes and increased utilization of formal and informal networks. Students are required to take—and pay tuition for—three or more courses to complete the PSSSP certificate in addition to the requirements for their degree program. In order to reduce the burden on students we have evaluated the content of courses and reduced the total number of required courses by combining the content of two courses into one whenever possible.

The immersion course that is taught in Mexico has been critical to helping students understand cultural differences and improve Spanish proficiency. However, the travel expenses associated with the immersion course are a burden for many students. We have created an alternative course for students who cannot afford the immersion course but it is not replicate of the cultural and language learning provided by the immersion course. We strive to keep costs to a minimum by choosing locations associated with lower airfare and lodging expenses and reducing the number of days of the course. Other options may be creating an immersion like experience closer to home. We are considering locations nationwide where large immigration waves from Latin American countries have settled including the states of California, Florida, and New York or even Puerto Rico. Another idea is to have students staying together in one location and using only the second language throughout the training period, which we have done when offering the training in intensive summer institutes.

Throughout the development of the program, we have struggled with ethical dilemmas when providing mental health services in more than one language. As mentioned earlier students and professionals who feel less competent in their second language may have to choose between denying services or working with less confidence and competence. Training programs and agencies who do not have supervisors with proficiency in a second language may have to decide whether to allow trainees or staff to provide services without adequate supervision. Programs that provide training for professionals, who will work in areas of the world with few resources, may not have the expertise or materials in the languages that will be used by their trainees. While there are no easy answers to these dilemmas, awareness of the dilemmas and open discussions of who to mitigate negative affects is a first step.

Conclusions

Mere conversational proficiency in a language is not sufficient for competent mental health services in that language. Professionals who intend to practice in a language other than the language they were trained in need training to bridge the gap between conversational fluency and professional proficiency.

We believe that the PSSSP program, with its focus on both cultural and linguistic competency could be adapted for use with other languages and cultures. The use of multilingual training teams can help trainees navigate the complexities and dilemmas presented when working with multiple languages.

References

Aguirre, C. (2004). One Latina's path through marriage and family therapy training. *Journal of Feminist Family Therapy, 16*(1), 1–17.
Ali, R. K. (2004). Bilingualism and systemic psychotherapy: Some formulations and explorations. *Journal of Family Therapy, 26*, 340–357.
Biever, J. L., Castaño, M. T., de las Fuentes, C., González, C., Servín-López, S., Sprowls, C., & Tripp, C. (2002). The role of language in training psychologists to work with Hispanic clients. *Professional Psychology: Research and Practice, 33*, 330–336.
Biever, J. L., Gómez, J. P., González, C. G., & Patrizio, M. (2011). Psychological services to Spanish-Speaking populations: A model curriculum for training competent professionals. *Training and Education in Professional Psychology, 5*, 81–87. doi:10.1037/a0023535.
Caldwell-Harris, C. L. (2014). Emotionality differences between a native and foreign language: Theoretical implications. *Frontiers in Psychology, 5*, 1–4. doi:10.3389/fpsyg.2014.01055.
Castaño, M. T., Biever, J. L., González, C. G., & Anderson, K. B. (2007). Challenges of providing mental health services in Spanish. *Professional Psychology: Research and Practice, 38*, 66–673. doi:10.1037/0735-7028.38.6.667.
Cummins, J. (1984). *Bilingualism and special education: Issues in assessment and pedagogy*. Clevedon, England: Multilingual Matters Ltd.
Guttfreund, D. G. (1990). Effects of language usage on the emotional experience of Spanish-English and English-Spanish bilinguals. *Journal of Consulting and Clinical Psychology, 58*, 604–607.
Marian, V., & Neisser, U. (2000). Language-dependent recall of autobiographical memories. *Journal of Experimental Psychology: General, 129*, 361–368.
Santiago-Rivera, A. L., & Altarriba, J. (2002). The role of language in therapy with the Spanish-English bilingual client. *Professional Psychology: Research and Practice, 33*, 30–38.
Santiago-Rivera, A., Altarriba, J., Poll, N., Gonzalez-Miller, N., & Cragun, C. (2009). Therapists' views on working with bilingual Spanish-English speaking clients: A qualitative investigation. *Professional Psychology: Research and Practice, 40*, 436–443.
Schrauf, R. W., & Rubin, D. C. (2000). Internal languages of retrieval: The bilingual encoding of memories for the personal past. *Memory & Cognition, 28*, 616–623.
Schwartz, A. L., Domenech Rodríguez, M. M., Santiago-Rivera, A. L., Arredondo, P., & Field, L. D. (2010). Cultural and linguistic competence: Welcome challenges from successful diversification. *Professional Psychology: Research and Practice, 41*, 210–222. doi:10.1037/a0019447.
Softas-Nall, L., Cardona, B., & Barritt, J. (2015). Challenges and diversity issues working with multilingual and bilingual couples and families: Implications for counseling. *The Family*

Journal: Counseling and Therapy for Couples and Families, 23(1), 13–17. doi:10.1177/1066480714548402.

Tehrani, N., & Vaughan, S. (2009). Lost in translation—using bilingual differences to increase emotional mastery following bullying. *Counselling and Psychotherapy Research, 9*, 11–17. doi:10.1080/14733140802656131.

Valdés, G., & Figueroa, R. A. (1994). *Bilingualism and testing: A special case of bias.* Norwood, NJ: Ablex.

Verdinelli, S., & Biever, J. L. (2009a). Experiences of Spanish/English bilingual supervisees. *Psychotherapy, 46*, 158–170. doi:10.1037/a0016024.

Verdinelli, S., & Biever, J. L. (2009b). Spanish-English bilingual psychotherapists: Personal and professional language development and use. *Cultural Diversity and Ethnic Minority Psychology, 15*, 230–242. doi: 10.1037/a0015111.

Verdinelli, S., & Biever, J. L. (2013). Therapists' experiences of cross-ethnic therapy with Spanish-speaking Latina/o clients. *Journal of Latina/o Psychology, 1*, 227–242. doi:10.1037/lat0000004.

Family Therapy in Postwar Kosova: Reforming Cultural Values in New Family Dynamics

Mimoza Shahini, Adelina Ahmeti and Laurie L. Charlés

Introduction

On March 24, 1999, the United States, together with the North Atlantic Alliance, NATO, started air strikes against Yugoslav military targets. During the 78-day air strike, in particular during March, Serbian army and paramilitary troops forced nearly one million Albanians to leave their homes—650,000 of them fled to Albania and hundreds of thousands to Macedonia. 10,533 Albanians went missing or were killed; 10,000 women were raped, and major material damage was caused during the 1998–1999 war.

Postwar Kosova has gone through changes that have been very difficult for families and their communities to understand. The war has resulted in a new definition of family. Finding new meaning to the collective trauma after a war remains a challenge for family members who have experienced human rights violations, including rape, forced displacement, murder in front of family members, and separation of men from women in lineups. It is our experience that the postwar context in Kosova has forced the inadvertent reformation of cultural dynamics.

In this chapter, we discuss some examples from our family therapy clinical work, training, and supervision experiences in Kosova. The first two authors are family therapy trained child psychiatrists living and working in Prishtina; the third author is a U.S. based family therapist who has traveled and worked with the two lead authors in Prishtina, training psychiatrists and psychologists, since 2010. In each of our countries, we provide family therapy services, family therapy supervision, and

---

M. Shahini (✉) · A. Ahmeti
Child and Adolescent Psychiatry Center of Prishtina, Pristina, Kosova

L.L. Charlés
Our Lady of the Lake University, San Antonio, USA

© American Family Therapy Academy 2016
L.L. Charlés and G. Samarasinghe (eds.), *Family Therapy in Global Humanitarian Contexts*, AFTA SpringerBriefs in Family Therapy,
DOI 10.1007/978-3-319-39271-4_6

family therapy consultation. When working together, however, we have provided training and consultation/supervision to family therapy trainees and client families in Kosova. In this chapter, that is our focus.

Kosova Context

Kosova is the newest independent country in Southeastern Europe, located in the center of the Balkan Peninsula, with an area of 10,887 km^2. It has a population of 1.8 million inhabitants, the majority of them Albanians, while the others are Serbs, Turks, Bosniacs, Roma, Ashkali, Egyptians and Gorani. In 1990, Kosova was proclaimed a republic and in 1991, an independent state. However, Kosova citizens could not enjoy independence because of Serbian regime, which lasted for a decade (1989–1999). During this decade, Albanian employees in the public sector were dismissed; schools and the university in the Albanian language were closed; the Albanian media, the TV channel and print media were shut down. Thousands of Albanians were imprisoned. Hundreds were forced to leave the country and seek asylum in Western European states.

During the 1990s Albanian associations in exile established the Kosova Liberation Army (KLA). Fierce fighting among the KLA and Serbian army and paramilitary forces began in 1998, when civilians were the most endangered population. There were massacres in 1999—the civilian population, including children, the elderly, and women—were massacred by Serbian forces. Some of the massacres were witnessed by the Organization for Security and Cooperation in Europe (OSCE).

In the new context of economic, political and social changes created in Kosova, there is embedded in the society a population that experienced severe traumas of war, including grave violations of human rights: rape, murder, deportation, destruction of property, and disappearance of loved ones. Mental health professionals—in this case only psychiatrists, since psychologists and counselors were almost nonexistent—had to offer professional help without proper qualifications for working with families. Previously in Kosova, education of general practitioners and psychiatrists has been oriented to "the individual patient" more than the family.

Providing assistance without a professional qualification is only one of the challenges for professionals in Kosova. For families the priority is establishing secure living conditions; treating psychological problems is not the main priority for the majority of them. "At this moment it is important for me that my child does not lack food and other basic things, because I am an adult and the child is not to be blamed for my traumas," one mother told us. Her 9-year-old son and several other family members were killed during the war.

Family Approach in Our Postwar Context

Post-war Kosova has been involved in a deep process of reformulating cultural values after the war. Family members have survived the war only to face transition processes that result in a drastic change of roles or status. We have observed in our work that if these changes are too sudden, or out of the family's control, then the health and psychological well-being of its members are inevitably affected. Herman (2007) talks about how traumatic incidents inhibit one's ability to act; one becomes unable to address injustice. A lack of control, or sense of control, about the rapidly changed family roles results in new, sometimes problematic, family dynamics.

Atrocities strongly affect the human psyche, at times hindering the ability to retell experience. In Kosova, this has been especially challenging because at the same time, the attitude of Kosovar families during and since the war, about the war, is quite stoic. For example, immediately after the year when professionals approached families, in a number of cases they faced an unspoken language, guarded fanatically within the family. This may result in particularly protective measures in a family. As one client stated:

> We have removed from our sight everything that is related to our murdered brothers; all the photographs, books and other things. We make sure we do not talk about them in front of children, because we do not want to upset them...

Historically, Kosovars' extended family, a structure that was respected by all the members and at the same time paved the way for communication, was based on a hierarchy of roles seen as a necessity for the family's survival. Yet that hierarchy disappeared or disintegrated as a result of the war. What are the challenges in a post-war country that the systemic family approach is particularly adept at addressing? In a situation of need for survival, the family gets organized in order to provide food and clothing, to the exclusion of psychological well-being. For a family therapist or professional who offers support, it is important to understand that this prioritization is legitimate and that intervention should focus on *integrating* psychological well-being with material needs.

As the first two authors also lived through the war, we understand personally as well as professionally what our clients tell us. It is understandable that a family that fails to obtain optimum physiological needs will find it difficult to address issues of psychological well-being. This is especially so for families that lost their property, had their property ownership documents lost or burnt, or whose members went missing. The therapist plays a significant role in creating an environment that allows the family to transcend the limits of physical survival and, in a natural manner, promote the open discussion on psychological needs while respecting the family's temporary limitations. Support and encouragement, while relying on existing capabilities and skills, can facilitate an optimistic outlook and healthy adaptation (Walsh 2007).

An important aspect for training professionals in family therapy in Kosova is how to help families to strengthen the values that enhance family cohesion and at the same time allow individuals to get used to the processes that a post-war situation brings. Family therapists should be aware of the processes that support members of families facing trauma, though at first these processes may look dysfunctional. For example, in our work, we routinely see changes in the balance of individuals' needs within the family, as in roles and responsibilities, is natural even though they may not be natural in another context that is seen as unrelated to or disconnected from the war.

Yet, for us, these changes in the family balance are a direct result of the war. For example, in many families that lost male members, the male role shifted naturally to young boys of the family, and in many cases to the lady of the house. To a therapist who was raised in a culture like that of Kosova, this shift might not coincide with prevailing beliefs, since the role as head of the family belongs only to men (husbands or their fathers). Thus the situation can be perceived as unnatural. After the war, the line between what was natural and unnatural became blurred.

We have found particular challenges in working the changing roles of former combatants, and the intergenerational dynamics changing between parents who survived the war, and their adolescent children who have no memory of it. We focus on this in the next section.

Case of Ex-combatant Families

An important aspect of training in family therapy is recognizing the reaction dynamics of families in a post-war situation, especially the families of ex-combatants. A frequent example in our family clinical practice is that of war veterans' families, who must be viewed clinically inclusive of the general context, rather than separate from it. For example, right after the war, the veterans' families faced multiple problems such as survival and also social pressure. War veterans joined the war willingly, with the aim of gaining state independence for Kosova. Yet the majority of them were not trained for combat. Some of them held guns for the first time. Studies after the war in Kosova show that a large percentage of the population had mental health problems, while many of them witnessed or participated in severe traumatic events (Wenzel et al. 2009).

Kosova war veterans have experienced or witnessed serious traumatic events. It is inevitable to connect their experience of war with their lives immediately after the war. Veterans returned to their families with a great sense of pride for what they had achieved, yet immediately faced social and political pressure over what had happened during the war. Many of them were stigmatized because of international pressure against war crimes—the same social treatment meted out to everyone. Due to many factors (insufficient budget, other state priorities, few organizations for the protection of veterans, lack of specialized services), veterans of the Kosova war were not provided proper financial, psychological and moral support when they returned from the war.

EXAMPLE A common phenomenon in our culture is to name a newborn baby after a close relative who died or was massacred and killed during the war, aiming to glorify, and honor the relative or his values. In one case we worked with, a father brought his 12 year old daughter for family therapy; he had been exhibiting severe symptoms consistent with PTSD and in the family session, explained the following. "I have a second family. My first four children and my wife were all killed by the Serbian police in a massacre, when I was a soldier. After the war, I remarried, and now, I have the same children as before." When I (AA) asked him to explain what he meant, he stated that he had named his new children the same names as the other children. The new, second, family was also two boys, and two girls. The father lived with the memory of two families; he kept photos of the dead children in the house; the living children were also a living memorial to the first family. Further, he had ascribed the same values, i.e. personal qualities, to the new, living children, which he had identified in the deceased children. In cases like this, we often find the way the former combatant has processed the memory of the traumatic incidents of the war has significantly influenced, unbeknownst to him, the issues that his current family configuration faces.

EXAMPLE Veterans we work with in Kosova may have been forced to cultivate a stoic sense of heroism and devotion to the homeland, but many of them are not able to convey what they really feel concerning the reality: the goal of protecting their family and in particular, their children. Many veterans' families remained without institutional support. They ensured the survival of their family with great difficulty. Our assumption is that they developed an unspoken language that protected them from social pressure but at the same time helped make a distinction between reality and their interior world. This attitude did not allow them to convey to their children what they really experienced during the war and at the same time could not convey what they were and what they are to this country. As one of our clients in treatment, a mother, stated:

> I do not care about my life any longer. I am very interested for my son and my husband to have good relations. My husband is struggling a lot to fulfill all the needs of our son, within the possibilities that we have. I know that he is nervous because he has suffered a lot during the war. He was kidnapped and has experienced terrible things, but he is wise; he never speaks in front of the children about what he has experienced; he constantly tries to stay calm and happy so that they would not be sad. Our son is an excellent student; he is very obedient and never causes us any problems, and I do not understand why he has those symptoms (obsessions and compulsions). My family has helped us a lot; they bought us an apartment because they knew that my husband is unable to work and they have much respect for him because he has sacrificed for this country. I often say to the children they should be grateful to my family and that when they grow up they must never forget this favor they have done to us.

EXAMPLE One element that may have also influenced the stoic attitude of veterans we work with is the fact that every day the media broadcast a commemorative day for those who were killed; often, such days are manipulated by politicians for their own interests. To a veteran who went to war knowing he might get killed, such days may have a negative impact rather than a positive one. In many cases we have seen, the veterans wished they had died during the war, or they have profound guilt feelings for surviving. Another of our clients, a former combatant, told us:

> Every day something happens that reminds me of war. My life has become unbearable. Nothing makes sense anymore, and I do not know what the meaning of my life is. I often wish I died during the war so I would not have to experience what I am experiencing today. Often I visit the grave of my close friend who was killed in the battle and I speak to him. I am disappointed with the reality and sometimes I have the feeling that their blood was not rewarded. When I see on television some people who go to lay flowers at the cemetery on commemoration days, I say it was better that I had died than see what I am seeing.

The shift in balance of the husband who is a former combatant has systemic repercussions on his family, and in particular, his marriage. In Kosova, in a family filled with unspoken language, the person who tries to maintain a balance is the wife. But we have seen wives spend so much energy solving such problems that they have no opportunity to deal with themselves, their own concerns. Wives of veterans' children say to us often that their life is not important; it is important to see their husband being happy and to fulfill their children's needs. A traumatized veteran retains the important role he takes from tradition at first glance (head of the family, but only figuratively), but in fact what we see is that the wife plays that role (head of the family, but without visible position), thus shouldering an additional burden.

Case of Parents and Their Adolescent Children: Postwar Families

In Kosova, at the Mental Health Center for Children and Adolescent—University Clinical Center in Prishtina, we have introduced a family approach where the first two authors, both family therapy trained child psychiatrists, perform psychiatric as well as family therapy consultations. Referrals or suggestions come from GPs, pediatricians or other health professionals, and from schools. In our clinic we also have many self-suggested cases: Families come with a clear goal—to solve the problem of the child—initially the family approach can be seen as the labeling of the family and the family members might feel as if they were the cause of the problem. Therefore, therapists we are careful not to present ourselves as a "family remedy" but to naturally explain what this approach is and how it helps the family to strengthen their potentials and not be blamed for what happens.

In general, we (MS and AA) first noticed that parents bring children because of various problems, such as anxiety, depression, ADHD, studying problems, behavior disorders and other problems. However, the three of us together (MS, AA, LLC) noted and discussed during our working sessions in Prishtina, a type of pattern to the types of issues raised in this family configuration. One of these patterns has to do with the relationships between adolescents born during or shortly after the war, and their parents, who lived through it. Here we briefly present two case examples, in which Dr. Ahmeti was the clinician, and Drs. Shahini and Charlés consultants.

CASE EXAMPLE: "TAKE ME WHERE THERE IS NO NOISE AT ALL"
Rrita[1] first came to therapy with her mother at age 14, after a suicide attempt with medication. Once she was no longer in crisis, I (AA) began to see her separately in addition to providing family therapy. One day, although two hours late to the session, Rrita arrived in a very good mood. The mother told me that the last session had had a good impact on Rrita. During that session I had noticed that Rrita had a need to talk about her past. She said that last year her father had beaten her severely when he found out that she likes a boy. Although Rrita was still seeing boys, the beatings had stopped: "Since I took the pills he is being more careful with me," Rrita said.

Rrita's behavior, especially a suicide attempt, seemed to be not very in line with the "stoic" approach to problems as common to her parent's generation. Rrita was also traumatized as she had seen her mother physically mistreated by her husband. Further, Rrita's uncle had died of an illness two years earlier; she was very close to him. There was also discord in the home between the generations living there, and resulting in disrupted, unstable living situation. Rrita told me: "My grandparents do not like my mother and very often they force us to leave the home. My father will come for us, eventually, but I am still mad at my father because he did not care enough about us."

Additionally, Rrita had discovered her father, a war veteran, was also having a romantic relationship outside the marriage. When I asked her if she had talked to her father, about how she felt of his behavior she told me: "One morning I told him 'you have changed on the phone the name of the woman you are meeting', and he said: 'You are talking too much.'" Rrita's suicide attempt occurred shortly afterward.

In the beginning of our work, Rrita had described feeling guilty, depressed, and apathetic. She had little emotional expression when she spoke, and in the first few sessions she had been talking very little and basically she was giving short answers. She told me she didn't want to live, nor did she want to stay with others. Instead, she said: "I want to stay in dark narrow places, where there is no noise at all." In the month before her suicide attempt, she told me she has been worrying more and stays only in dark places, such as behind the sofa or under the table. "Since the 7th grade I started staying alone, I couldn't bear the noise …."

Perhaps, the "noise" had symbolic meaning to Rrita, as if she was not able to be stoic about her suffering, nor her family's. However, when talk of her future came up, she lit up. Rrita, extremely intelligent, said she would like "to study medicine, to be away from these people in my family, to go to a course of dancing, learn foreign languages, to adopt a child and offer him/her all the things I did not have during my childhood." When I asked her what she liked the most about the sessions, she said she was happy that she could talk to me about her future because she never had the

---
[1]Names have been changed.

opportunity to talk to anyone about it. Her mother had noticed changes since the first session, and was very thankful. She says her daughter has changed a lot especially since the last session. But her father did not want to accept this. At the last session he did not come to the clinic with them, saying he had things to do.

CASE EXAMPLE: "LEAVING AND NEVER COMING BACK" Venera, 16 years old and born in Prishtina, was referred by her mother because Venera was missing from home, and also, missing school. Venera's mother knew her daughter smoked, but her real fear: "I'm afraid maybe she uses a drug." Venera lived in a family with her parents, and four siblings, all older than she is (in their mid-late twenties) and working or studying in the city. Venera's father is the second boy from the six children in his family. During the war he has been a helper in army. One of his brothers had died during the war, killed by Serbian military; two sons of his aunt were also killed. From that period of time he has become very nervous; he has seen lots of people massacred during the war. Now, he only works at his job and he doesn't do anything in the household. He has been diagnosed with PTSD.

Soon Venera's mother revealed other fears about her daughter. Venera, fluent in English and German, is also quite beautiful. She worked as a model for one company and she often stayed all night with the production team on jobs. Venera's mother became more preoccupied about her because recently she had seen Venera with an older woman, and later, found in Venera's bag a letter in which Venera has written the phrase "love lesbian." Venera's mother was very religious; praying five times a day. She stated she is terrified because, as she put it, "If my husband and oldest son know about this behavior they will kill Venera, because this is a shame for our family."

Venera, in two or three sessions we met, described how she liked to be in the company with girls. She has her girlfriends from Prishtina and also a nearby city. In the interim between sessions, she had run away from school and met with her girlfriends and also with other girls, repeatedly. She had spent weeks out of the house. When she returned, her elder brother beat her, but she again left to have contact with those girls. Venera has an aunt in Europe, who is lesbian. She says in one session, "I hate my family. Why they don't support me? When I become 18 years old I will go to live in foreign country."

Case Discussion

The differences between generations remain closed or unspoken, as a way we believe reflects traditional Kosovar's family values of non-destruction and cohesion. Yet the differences of family dynamics of how to do this becomes even more poignant in post-war cases, when there is more suffering, feelings of revenge, or feelings of victimization, all hidden in the family system. Many families may not be conscious of the implications of war trauma on their family; or, it may be the opposite, when everything is attributed to the war. Either way, their present dynamics are unclear to them.

Those present dynamics are drastically different for families with intergenerational extended members in the same household. This type of household is very typical in Kosova. While intergenerational households existed before the war, now —after the war—the dynamics seem to be more open to comment or act upon when they become problematic. They are seen as more of a problem. Additionally, for the families we see, each generation (all in the same household) has a distinct narrative about the war. For the parents, who survived it, it is a stoic acceptance or denial, a hope to return to the old family dynamics, or adjustment to the changed family life. For adolescents, particularly those who are exactly the age of the end of the war (15 or 16), there is no memory of the war, no interest in a return to family dynamics they never experienced, and rather, a focus on the future rather than the past. It is not surprising that Venera wants to leave to a foreign country; she is representative of many people her age in Kosova. Kosova has the youngest population in Europe; over 53 % of the population is under age 25[2]; the youth unemployment rate for this population in 2014 was 61 %.[3]

Strengthening a family in such a situation is easier than it sounds. Because of the hierarchy order in family communication it is difficult to establish open communication between children and parents. For example, extended families in Kosova must often have validation of the head of the family, who in the majority of cases is the eldest person, yet who may have little awareness of the families' changed dynamics. Further, it remains a particular challenge to have open discussion in pairs, especially problems related to privacy among generations living together. For example, we see this when a wife has problems with a mother in-law. In our culture, traditionally, this type of problem is not spoken about with foreign persons (i.e. a therapist) or with extended family, because it could increase the problem between the spouses. Similarly, families often do not wish to include or involve other institutions, such as schools, or place of work, in supporting the therapist's systemic approach. The reason for this is due to stigma.

For a family therapist or professional who offers support, we suggest that trainees work hard to understand how families are prioritizing their needs is legitimate and that intervention should focus on *integrating* psychological well-being with material needs. This is different from an individual approach because as family therapy trainers we want therapists to create an environment that allows the family, as a collective, to transcend the limits of physical survival, and deal with the aftereffects of the war. We train clinicians to use various family therapy methods, but in as natural a manner as possible, and with respect to the culture in Kosova. We focus trainees' awareness of how to promote open discussion on psychological needs while respecting the family's temporary limitations. Support and encouragement,

---

[2]Assistance to Kosovo: Education for the Future, European Commission. Retrieved at http://eeas.europa.eu/delegations/kosovo/documents/press_corner/education_for_the_future_en.pdf.

[3]Republic of Kosova, Office of the Prime Minister, Kosovo Agency of Statistics. Retrieved at: https://ask.rks-gov.net/eng/.

while relying on existing capabilities and skills, can facilitate an optimistic outlook and healthy adaptation (Walsh 2007).

We encourage trainees to pay attention to the changes in the balance of individuals' needs within the family, in their roles and responsibilities. We also try to help them see family needs as natural, and often, connected and related to their experience of war. For the therapists we train in Prishtina, we take care to teach them not to present ourselves as a "family remedy" but to naturally explain what this approach is and how it can help the family to strengthen their potentials and not be blamed for what happens.

Reflections on Family Therapy Training Programs in Kosova

Family therapy training origins in Kosova began in the first after-war years (1999), when mental health professionals were introduced to the concept of family therapy through Kosova Family Professional Education Collaborative project, which helped train and develop family and community-based mental health services (Griffith et al. 2005). Members of the American Family Therapy Academy (AFTA), based in the U.S., participated in this collaborative. At that time, local psychiatrists (including the first author) were introduced to different family approaches, with a special focus on the reconciliation and recovery process.

As the cooperation deepened, the first author received an invitation to be key plenary speaker at the 2009 International Family Therapy Association (IFTA) Congress in Portoroz, Slovenia. That plenary resulted in an opportunity to discuss with the IFTA Board a training collaboration with Kosova, aiming to build a specialization program of family therapy in Kosova. The idea was presented to KFT, a non-governmental organization in Prishtina, which provided financial support for four years of the program.

As a cumulative result of all these combined resources, and the financial and moral commitment of Kosovars, Albanians, and members of the family therapy community across the globe, Kosova now has established the Counseling and Family Therapy program, a Master's of Arts Degree, at Dardania College, in the heart of Prishtina. At first partially involving international trainers (including the third author, among others), the graduate teaching in Family Therapy coursework is primarily taught by local professionals, such as the first two authors.

ROLE OF THE INTERNATIONAL COMMUNITY The two lead authors, who lived in Prishtina full time during and since the war, have observed that although a large number of organizations worked with families in the field in Kosova, often this work was neither documented nor coordinated with local institutions, and did not ensure continuity of those services. Worse, a good part of those services offered to families in Kosova were discontinued as soon as the situation in the country was no longer profitable for some organizations, or, when it ceased to be a topic of international interest.

Nevertheless, in our experience, the use of external professional resources (co-operation with universities, organizations that have professionals in the family therapy area) is necessary in order to pass knowledge from international to local professionals. This knowledge passing helps to maintain the standards necessary for a proper education in family therapy and is critical for a project's sustainability.

The establishment of a sustainable system between humanitarian organizations and state institutions must be a priority issue for a country; yet, in Kosova we have found this to be a challenge. Additionally, professional colleagues of ours in Kosova involved in work with families have faced further individual challenges after their family therapy training. These include the lack of supervision to the lack of opportunities within the country to pursue specialization or training in family therapy. Meanwhile, the professionals who did have an opportunity to access book information in foreign languages (whether in Kosova borders or outside of it) faced another challenge: adapting the book family therapy they learned to the real life mentality of Kosova families.

The role of the international community has been critical to the development of family therapy in Kosova. The use of human resources and capacity building provided by humanitarian organizations reduces the high cost of training for family counselors and therapists, especially in low and middle-income countries, but particularly for those reconstructing after war. Involvement of local staff in the activities of humanitarian organizations is also an opportunity for mutual benefit. Locals have no language barriers; locals know the culture; locals have assets and resources that outsiders do not have (nor can ever acquire). Local people can be supervised by foreigners and at the same time gain clinical experience with international expatriates working for those organizations (This is in fact how the authors met each other).

We have found this practice significant for us in the family therapy training we have been part of in Kosova over the past years. Local organizations should be strengthened to maintain standards of education and create strong links with international organizations to consolidate the family therapy program and take advantage of opportunities for continuous professional training, especially in countries where family therapy is being developed. Local involvement at every stage of programming is critical. This does not mean that the training should not respect the necessary standards set by international organizations that define licensing criteria, but they should be flexible in adapting theory to the context therapists are going to apply.

In a country like Kosova, or any other country with limited budgetary resources, it is important that the training be addressed to local resources and be developed internally. Training projects should select people who are motivated in their profession and in particular those who have the opportunity to have contact with families. Certainly the introduction of family therapy might be a novelty for professionals, such as psychologists or psychiatrists, but novelty is not enough to maintain their motivation for training. It is necessary for professionals to have contact with families in order to practice the knowledge they gain during training and be able to understand and experience the dynamics of family sessions as well as their effects. This is especially true in low-income countries, where such a profession is non-profitable; in such places, it is highly unlikely that persons who are trained will continue after completion of the training.

Our experience of the development of family therapy in Kosova has been rewarding, yet challenging. We have developed deep professional relationships and increased our skill set such that the first two authors are now trainers of family therapy for our colleagues in the country. For the third author, the work over the years in Kosova provided incredible lessons that were taken to other training projects in other conflict-affected countries.

In our view, family is the most important place to start the process of reconciliation after a war, especially when the whole community has been involved in collective trauma. Notwithstanding the difficulties, it seems that the number of families who are looking to have a family approach has been increasing. This approach is presented with care and respect of family values to every family involved in therapy. Yet at the same time, we often use psycho education with members of the family. Constantly, we encourage new therapists to focus on family strengths, as we believe it empowers the family to deal with problems with as little pain. We are aware that mentality of the family, and their life before the war, cannot be replaced, but, after the war, we work together with families to identify points less painful so that they can go on.

References

Griffith, J. L., Agani, F., Weine, S., Ukshini, S., Pulleyblank Coffey, E., Ulaj, J., et al. (2005). A family-based mental health program of recovery from state terror in Kosova. *Behavioral Sciences & the Law, 23*(4), 547–558.

Herman, J. (2007). *Trauma and recovery*. New York, NY: Basic Books.

Walsh, F. (2007). Traumatic loss and major disasters: Strengthening family and community resilience. *Family Process, 46*(2), 207–227.

Wenzel, T., Rushiti, F., Aghani, F., Diaconu, G., Maxhuni, B., & Zitterl, W. (2009). Suicidal ideation, post-traumatic stress and suicide statistics in Kosovo: An analysis five years after the war. *Suicidal ideation in Kosovo, Torture, 19*(3), 238–247.

Time, Trauma, and Ambiguous Loss: Working with Families with Missing Members in Postconflict Cyprus

Kyle D. Killian

Introduction

The other day, I took my car to the garage because the brakes were squeaking a lot. My mechanic told me, "Well, buddy, I couldn't repair your brakes, so I made your horn louder." There are times when I feel that we helping professionals are in the same business as the mechanic—we diagnose a problem, but are we helping our clients and their families to heal? We can identify "disorders", apply a sticky label—for instance, Post Traumatic Stress Disorder (PTSD)—but are we addressing our clients' challenges in a way that leads to healing and well-being from within their own cultural framework, from their perspective of what illness and wellness is all about? Or are we sending them out of the garage with a T-shirt that reads "PTSD diagnosis—don't make any sudden moves"?

In this chapter, I engage a crucial dimension of trauma, which is the disruption of the unifying thread of temporality, and the unique challenges presented by traumatic ambiguous loss. Trauma discourses propose that "symptoms" of traumatic stress, often referred to as dissociation and multiplicity, can be understood in terms of trauma's impact in disrupting the sense of being-in-time. Ambiguous loss, experienced by families with missing members in post-conflict zones, captures this freeze-frame, timeless quality of trauma, where traumatic experiences become an eternal present in which a family system and larger communities can feel trapped, and notions of a future lose meaning. The ways in which traumatic memory is both present and absent, elusively existing in the realms of the sensory and affective, and defying language and assimilation into a coherent sense of identity, are explored. Adapting family therapy practices to work with families with missing members in post-conflict Cyprus, and the complex ways that different members adjust and adapt

---

K.D. Killian (✉)
Capella University, 225 S. Sixth St., Ninth Floor, Minneapolis, MN 55402, USA
e-mail: Kyle.killian@capella.edu

© American Family Therapy Academy 2016
L.L. Charlés and G. Samarasinghe (eds.), *Family Therapy in Global Humanitarian Contexts*, AFTA SpringerBriefs in Family Therapy,
DOI 10.1007/978-3-319-39271-4_7

following DNA identification of remains, are discussed through a clinical vignette. I conclude with a brief discussion of the discourse of refugee trauma and the positionality of systemic practitioners who seek to be helpful to refugee families.

Defining and Deconstructing Terms: PTSD, Ambiguous Loss and Temporality

In the world of grief and mourning, *ambiguous loss* is one that defies closure, even within healthy families (Boss 2007). A family member can abruptly vanish *physically,* with no verification of whereabouts or fate as dead or alive, or a member fades away *psychologically* from dementia and other cognitive or emotional impairments that contribute to what I term *death of personality*. In either case, grief becomes complicated, not by some psychic weakness or some deficit or pathology in the family members, but from the profound complications of *loss shrouded in doubt* (Boss and Carnes 2012). Meaning is ruptured when a loved one is here but not here, or gone, but not for sure. The family as a whole, and the individuals in it, struggle as their story continues without an ending.

Endings in movies are typically marked by certainty, a clear resolution of tension between the protagonist and antagonist. In a word, Hollywood offers audiences *closure*. North American culture scores high on need for closure, with the vast majority of people craving certainty (Chirumbolo et al. 2004; Pierro et al. 2012); and so the idea that closure is impossible is frequently viewed as anathema, and vehemently resisted by moviegoers at the cinema (Killian 2015), and sometimes by clients and professionals in the therapy room. In real life, and in cases of ambiguous loss, closure is a myth (Boss and Carnes 2012). Even in cases of a validated death, there can be some ambiguity that "immobilizes and traumatizes" (Boss 2007, p. 106). This ambiguity also freezes the grief process, impeding cognition, and blocking coping skills and decision-making processes (Boss 1999). Family members must create their own truth about the status of the person absent in mind or body. Without closure, members must live with the paradox of presence, and absence. I further explicate the phenomena of frozen grief, and foreclosed future, through a discussion of trauma's relation to *temporality*.

First, Post-Traumatic Stress Disorder is a problematic diagnostic category, for two reasons: (1) it pathologizes a normal reaction to prolonged and traumatic events, and (2) the stresses associated with many unresolved events produce a profound discontinuity (losing one's home, community, etc.), but also can represent continuing conditions or circumstances ("I was not a refugee, I became a refugee, I am still a refugee"). William Faulkner wrote, "The past is never dead. *It's not even past*." Second, trauma survivors experience an interesting mix of remembering and not remembering; they often report vivid re-experiencing of the traumatic event, or "flashbacks", and nightmares and recurrent memories, but at the same time, crucial aspects of traumatic events are often repressed (Mather and Marsden 2004). In a sort of "tip of the tongue" phenomenon, one can *almost* remember an aspect of the event, but it escapes consciousness at the last instant. In such cases,

> instead of flashbacks, the past remains "inaccessible" to present consciousness. Here its failure to present itself is signalled unconsciously in a series of "symbolic" symptoms that defy explanation at the level of rational consciousness. In this respect, PTSD, like postmodern temporality, challenges the Kantian assumption that coherent self-consciousness is the necessary condition of human experience....the symptomatology of experiential fragmentation, seems to occupy the far end of the continuum that could be called, for lack of a better term, "normal" experience (Mather and Marsden 2004, p. 206).

But traumatic memory, like ambiguous loss, can be a trickster—it can be both present and absent, elusively existing in the realms of the sensory and affective, but defying language and assimilation into a coherent sense of identity.

Another crucial dimension of trauma is the breaking up of the unifying thread of temporality (Stolorow 2003). "[C]linical features usually described as dissociation and multiplicity can be understood in terms of trauma's impact in disrupting the sense of being-in-time" (Stolorow 2003, p. 158). Psychological trauma represents a "shattering of one's experiential world—in particular, of those 'absolutisms' that allow one to experience one's world as stable, predictable, and safe, and oneself as inviolable" (Stolorow 2003, p. 159):

> Torn from the communal fabric of being-in-time, traumatic loss remains insulated from human dialogue. In the region of trauma, all duration or stretching along collapses, past becomes present, and future loses all meaning other than endless repetition. In this sense it is trauma, not the unconscious, that is *timeless* (Stolorow 2003, p. 160).

In this timeless region, it may be useful, to varying degrees for family members, to think in a both/and fashion, or dialectically, about the loss—"my loved one is gone, but s/he is also here; I can tolerate the stress of ambiguity" (Boss 2007). This can be a source of resilience in an overwhelming, ongoing situation with seemingly no end. As Fuchs (2005) asserts:

> [T]he future appears as a "not yet" or "yet to come", experienced as the temporality of awaiting, striving, or longing for...time is experienced explicitly, but now as moving on relentlessly and separating us from the lost person. The gap to the past may not be bridged anymore: this is the temporality of missing or mourning. In both cases, explicit time arises as a negation of implicit or lived time; "it is experienced as a "not yet" or "no more", with a component of...suffering (p. 195).

Fuchs (2005) also posits that a slowing, or retardation, in one's sense of time is associated with growing distress and suffering, seen in constellations of symptoms commonly referred to as major depression, traumatic stress, or severe cases of ambiguous loss. This slowing of time:

> may be regarded as a complete desynchronization or un-coupling from intersubjective time. Here the individual becomes obsessed by the past, and loses the lived synchronicity with others....explicit time establishes a merciless rule: its passing by is noticed painfully, and the future of lived time seems closed forever (Fuchs 2005, p. 196).

Similarly on the social level, uncompleted tasks, unresolved conflicts, and experiences of survivor guilt, loss, or separation lead to a temporary disturbance or lasting loss of the lived synchrony with others. Thus, desynchronization is not only a biological process but a social one (Fuchs 2005, p. 196). It's not just in our heads, but out here in an ecology of social relations. "Optimal synchronization is equivalent to implicit or lived temporality: There is no gap or backlog between the state of the body and the surrounding processes" (Fuchs 2005, p. 196). As my colleague Siba Grovogui would say, it is "just in time", functioning in the implicit mode. "However, the living being periodically goes through states of imbalance, shortage and asynchrony that must be compensated for by some suitable behavior" (Fuchs 2005, p. 196).

Time as a Crucial Aspect of Agency

Mead (1932) proposed that "anticipating the novelty of every future demands that we create a novel orientation to the past" (p. 31, cited in Mattley 2002, p. 367). Family members may choose to idealize the missing member, or rationalize that the person was often psychologically or emotionally absent from them anyway, so this was just one more form of a "cheat". Thus, the past is not immutable—it is a shape shifter, molded according to a family's needs. Finally, notions of psychological health and illness cannot be understood in isolation from their social and political conditions of emergence (Mather and Marsden 2004, p. 208). It's noteworthy that PTSD is often thought of "in terms of 'signs' that do not 'communicate'" (Mather and Marsden 2004, p. 208). The sufferer of trauma or ambiguous loss is obliged to author a story that conceptualizes trauma as a "play of difference": from a noted absence of sensory fragments not yet present, to a presence inflected with absence (an incomplete narrative explaining what happened), to a personal narrative that fully reflects one's identity, occasionally buffeted by sensory fragments in the form of flashbacks (Mather and Marsden 2004, p. 217). Weaving a coherent narrative—a healing one—is no simple task, for client, or therapist.

Sociohistorical Context of Cyprus

I lived and worked in Cyprus for several years, am married to a Greek Cypriot refugee, and have a working knowledge of Greek. Displaced families are a part of my personal and professional communities in Cyprus, and I continue to provide pro-bono psychotherapy to families there. Located west of Lebanon and south of Turkey, Cyprus is the third largest island in the Mediterranean. Following a five-year, anti-colonial struggle, Cyprus gained its independence from Great Britain in 1960. The two main ethnic groups, the Greek Cypriots, 78 % of the population, and the Turkish Cypriots, about 18 %, struggled for power and representation in the fledgling government. Intercommunal violence between Greek and Turkish Cypriots erupted three years later, and again in 1964 and 1967. In 1974, a nationalist coup d'etat supported by Greece was followed by an invasion by Turkey that displaced approximately 275,000 persons from both communities and led to the de facto division of the island. United Nation's security forces and Green Line remain today, physically dividing the island into two parts. A lack of resolution to the Cyprus Problem has meant that no refugee family has returned to their home and possessions.

Gender, sexuality, class, race and (re)production were explicit factors in the modes of violence before and after 1960. Mass murders, rape as a weapon of war, and 1619 missing or "disappeared" Greek Cypriots were fixtures of the state's narrative of why they "should not forget" what was done to them at the hands of the "enemy." Since 2004, the humanitarian intervention by the UN Committee for Missing Persons (CMP) in locating and exhuming bodies from mass graves on the island (Yakinthou 2008) has reopened inquiry about the violence of nationalist powers and their contingent interests. Shifts in epistemological understandings are being sparked by a series of legal cases (e.g., Christofis Pashas and Charalambos Palmas) against the Republic of Cyprus for withholding information on the location of missing loved ones (Yakinthou 2008).

the missing

the way loss seeps
into neck hollows
and curls at temples
sits between front teeth
cavity

empty and waiting
for mourning to open
(Hammad 2001)

Hammad suggests that "the loss" does not go away, but sits there like a cavity waiting for mourning to open. The desire to come to some kind of "resolution" to the problem of the missing via forensic technology and DNA may represent a displacement of the larger social problem (i.e., the life and death of people within sovereign states). A 35-year-old, middle-class, displaced male Greek Cypriot speaks to the open wounds of a nation:

> Our nation has been wounded since 1974. Our people and our lands are lost in the hands of the Turks. As long as our missing [kin] is not given to us and our lands are not returned to us there is no way that this conflict can be resolved. Our duty is to have back what we lost and have been waiting for the last 27 years (Agathangelou and Killian 2009, pp. 29–30).

Drawing on DNA to locate the bones of the missing, the state depends on the medical establishment. But such technological interventions leave few "winners" behind. A 50-year-old Greek Cypriot woman shared the following about her missing husband:

The years are passing very fast. I am still waiting for him. Now, he has 5 grandchildren and I want him to see how they are beautiful like him. He is going to come. They did not find his bones after my sons gave their DNA. I feel as nobody cares and nobody knows of our pain and suffering behind closed doors. The black clothes I am wearing represent the blackness of my heart (Agathangelou and Killian 2009, p. 47).

The medical establishment takes DNA as "a tool" and uses it to participate in "intersubjective tasks" while promising "closure" about the problem of the missing. Giving DNA as the UN and the state expect in order to help "put to bed" the issue of the missing does not eradicate the displacements that people are facing daily, especially if they are struggling to make ends meet (Saoulli 2007; Yakinthou 2008).

Clinical Vignette

A Greek Cypriot family lost, and did not lose, their father in the 1974 war. He was serving in the army, and was one of the 1619 missing following the armed conflict. Narratives of the hero, the fallen, beloved husband, brother, father, uncle circulated in the extended family and larger communities of Greek Cyprus. A room in the family's home represented the frozen time associated with ambiguous loss, remaining unchanged for 30 years. Extended families tried to be supportive and helpful, but the unclear loss over time made it hard to find the right words to say to the family. Then, one day, remains were found. Brothers were asked to give DNA so the remains could be identified. One brother refused to give his DNA, ambivalent about receiving the results, and having the haze of ambiguity lifted and replaced with the blinding bright light of certainty, and permanent separation from his brother. A son provided his DNA, and the remains were positively identified. A missing member had been found. The family recalibrated to the news, but to what end? Resolution? Closure? Yes, and no. At the funeral, the sons and grandsons could finally mourn, relatives distant and close wailed and collapsed in the church, a community galvanized around commemoration of a brother in arms. The wife, now viewed a widow, could finally dismantle the room, which had been an altar to his memory. But like *Inception*, or a Harold Pinter play, there is a twist ending. I heard the widow whisper at the dinner table: "I know he met, and married a Turkish woman, and has a family *there* now...." Now she is a wife again, and a scorned one, at that. The narrative following ambiguous loss coheres for members in vastly different ways, based on their extent of re-synchronization, and desynchronization. The sons have touched their father's bones, and mourned his memory; they have buried him in the ground. Time moves forward, again. *But for the wife, the husband's bones will not stay buried.*

Discussion

Importance of Social Support and Gender

In the above vignette, the community sought to be supportive of the family with a missing member, but relationships can dissipate when friends and neighbors do not know what to say or do in the face of an ambiguous loss (Boss 2007, p. 106). Studies show that perceived community social support is significantly related to successful family adaptation in adjusting to stressful circumstances (McCubbin et al. 1996; Thompson et al. 1995). For example, perception of ample social support strongly predicted lower traumatic stress in Greek Cypriot refugee families (Agathangelou and Killian 2002, 2009), demonstrating that social support can "trump" severity of trauma, with highly traumatized but highly supported subjects reporting significantly less post-traumatic stress symptoms than those who were less severely traumatized but less socially supported. Agathangelou and Killian (2002) found that women reported significantly lower social support, indicating that this resource was not available to them to the extent that it was available to men. Why might this be? Findings from descriptive data suggest that men typically frequent the *kafeneia*, or coffee houses, in their local communities on a daily, and sometimes nightly, basis in Cyprus, and this provides a regular opportunity for both routine and sociopolitical conversation and watching sporting events. Having places to go and talk about daily and historical events may serve as a buffer to long-term maladaptation to trauma and may enhance a person's sense of well-being. "Understanding and meaning are cultural, public, and intersubjective" (Goolishian and Anderson 1992, p. 11). Mental space is a public space, public through labour and dialogue, and the self is always evolving out of this public space. However, patriarchy privileges men's power and control and does not bestow the same prerogatives to women. Men's social support at the kafeneia represents an access to a public space whereas there has been no parallel privilege, activity, or social outlet for women in Greek Cypriot culture, save for grassroots activism and bicommunal organizations (e.g., *Hands Across the Divide*).

Working with Internally Displaced Greek Cypriot Families

In the Western tradition of the helping professions, the prevailing view is that talking about traumatic experiences is the single most therapeutic behavior in which survivors can engage (Bolton 2000; Davis and Friedman 1985). However, the value of a "talking cure" has not been established in many cultures, and even in some European countries (e.g., Greece), counseling and therapy are taboo, with families not discussing personal problems with strangers (McGoldrick et al. 2005). Specifically in Cyprus, therapy is still not viewed as a viable option for many distressed families. Therefore, how can professionals approach the provision of services to refugee families in a contextually appropriate and effective manner?

Families may be more comfortable discussing their problems or symptoms with persons who describe themselves as priests, "doctors" or "healers" because, from their contextual perspective, visiting a psychiatrist or "shrink" is evidence of insanity (van der Veer 1998). Ethnicity, race and gender also frame people's ideas regarding the causes of their traumatic experiences and the context within which symptoms are evaluated. In Cyprus, women may have internalized the ideology that the protecting and caring for one's family is more crucial than one's own well-being. In this patriarchal context, Cypriot women may also view their own traumatic experiences as relatively unimportant and choose to ignore or deny symptoms. To avoid misinterpreting politeness as passivity, physical complaints as pathological somaticization, and an initial "trivial pursuit" as a sign of disingenuousness, culturally sensitive therapists refrain from jumping to conclusions informed solely by their own contextual frameworks.

Refugees may construe non-directive, more collaborative approaches as indicating a lack of competence or interest on the part of the practitioner (van der Veer 1998). Therefore, it may be helpful to reiterate one's treatment approach, to explain the purpose of particular questions, and to communicate repeatedly one's expectations of refugee clients. In turn, refugees themselves can be important sources of information about cultural differences and alternative ways of understanding the world and their own experiences.

In gathering sensitive information, therapists must be aware of the anxiety, shame, and/or embarrassment that are often associated with sexual coercion and the potential repercussions of its coming to light in front of other family members. A wife or mother may not want her husband or children to know they were sexually assaulted for a variety of reasons and may be loathe to discuss it in their presence. Gender can intersect with ethnicity, race, or nationality with women from traditional and explicitly patriarchal contexts being especially fearful of how others will react if they discover what has happened to them. Individual therapy sessions and group sessions with other women may provide opportunities for refugee women to discuss such experiences.

Promising avenues of intervention include trauma therapy, psychoeducation, relationship enhancement, and community activism. Educating families about normative emotional and psychological acute and long-term reactions to extreme stressors may provide the basic knowledge survivors need to develop alternative understandings of what has happened and how they can choose to respond to the trauma and its sequelae in the future. Therapists can describe traumatic stress symptoms in terms of relational dynamics frequently observed, such as emotional numbing and withdrawal. Over time, these strategies for avoiding painful intrusive thoughts and feelings connected with traumas dramatically diminish intimacy, self-disclosure, and skills for conflict resolution in couples and families. Systems in crisis can benefit from learning and implementing a variety of interpersonal skills (e.g., problem solving, conflict resolution) and enhancing personal resources (e.g., emotional self-awareness).

Important questions include "what happened and why," "why did I react the way I did," and "if something like this occurs again, how will I respond to it?" (Figley 1995). By listening to the recounting of traumatic events in a sensitive manner and offering constructive interpretations of the meaning of such events, families help reframe traumas and facilitate a movement towards a *healing theory* (Figley 1989) in which survivors can answer the preceding questions to their satisfaction. Therapists can help families connect with other families who have gone through similar experiences, especially families that can provide a sense of hope and a model of successful adaptation. Encouraging community cohesion in villages and towns in Cyprus enters the realm of grass roots organizing, activism, and public policy, and thus working with refugee families erodes the Western dichotomy between public and private; the two are inextricably linked.

A focus group of refugees (Agathangelou and Killian 2009) put forward that rather than expecting Cypriots to self-identify clinical needs and then get up and go to the offices of mental health professionals, the professionals could visit the communities in an outreach capacity and facilitate large group discussions there, basically creating the possibility of inquiring into those grey areas of social relations (i.e., healthy modes of living) and to disrupt the idea of them being "damaged goods". As the family is central to Cypriots, creating spaces in community settings where extended family members can discuss the vast changes that conflict, war, and even global changes have now brought and are bringing to their family system would be a more appropriate approach. Topics of discussion at such meetings might include the difficulties associated with losing one's continuity with the past through displacement from one's home, possessions, and community (Agathangelou and Killian 2002; Zetter 1999), the dissonance encountered at the nexus of the ethno-nationalist push to "NOT forget", the personal prohibitions of "I don't want to talk about it" or "I cannot burden my family with the terrible things only I experienced", and the familial injunctions, often from the next generation, of "Don't talk about the past/the war". It is hoped that such an outreach would create spaces for therapeutic witnessing (Papadopoulos 1996, 1998). In the context of "ordinary conversations" about unpleasant experiences, a therapist is present to listen with minimal facilitation as a "human witness", allowing persons to thaw trauma and reconnect various parts of their personal and collective narratives (Papadopoulos 1998). When people come together and engage in "ordinary" dialogue about events and experiences—both the ordinary and extraordinary—they can begin the process of regenerating a sense of trust, and in some circumstances shed what is often an illusory isolation in their traumatic experiences. It is through this process that the therapist comes together as a member of the community/ties s/he is part of, to collectively participate in the process of working with memory to defatalize the past and present, and open up alternative possibilities for a future once foreclosed.

Conclusion

Refugeedom is not ensconced exclusively in the discipline of psychology. It intersects political (including domestic and foreign policies), religious, ethnic, sociological, financial, and ecological dimensions (e.g. where refugee housing is constructed, etc.) (Papadopoulos 2001). An approach that takes into account these dimensions, and permits helping professionals to also locate themselves in the context of the service systems in which they belong is a politico-economic, systemic approach. As Papadopoulos (2001) asserts, "systemic approaches are useful in working with refugees because they can sharpen the professionals' epistemological sensitivity and inform them about the interaction of the various narratives that each one of these systems uses to express itself" (p. 406).

The narrative or discourse of the medical model (i.e., the "PTSD approach") is often incongruent with the lived experience of refugee families (Weine et al. 2004). While many Cypriot refugees appear to exhibit symptoms of traumatic stress (Agathangelou and Killian 2002), few Cypriot refugees view their experiences within a framework of diagnostic criteria, PTSD treatment, or a medical model of trauma and recovery. One Greek-Cypriot male, for example, who scored significantly above the "clinical cut-off score" for a diagnosis of PTSD, denied that war traumas played any role in his current state and situation. Conversations revealed that he had experienced a range of severe traumatic episodes, including interrogations and beatings while imprisoned by fellow Greek Cypriots, plus threats to his life, digging his own grave, and searching cemeteries for his missing, now confirmed dead brother. His chronic anxiety, anger, foreshortened sense of future, inability to hold a job, and a host of other problems and symptoms readily indicated a PTSD-like syndrome, but he and his family discounted any such clinical interpretations. In a context where family is the focal point (Agathangelou and Killian 2005), family members are more likely to see the manifestations and costs of war trauma through a family lens (Weine et al. 1997), and on a broader tapestry of significant life events.

What then constitutes a transformative process? Researchers (Ramirez-Esparza and Pennebaker 2006; Pennebaker and Seagal 1999) have examined the relationship between written disclosure (under secure and predictable conditions) of traumatic events and consequent physiological and psychological change. They found that participants in their study who chose to write about traumas showed an improvement in immunological functioning, greater reduction in subjective distress, and fewer health center visits than participants who wrote about trivial events. Furthermore, participants who included both "facts" and emotions around those "facts" were able to experience fewer health problems than those who included only the "facts." Thus, an alternative to simple medication or psychotherapy's "talking cure" might be the writing and/or story telling cure. In what contexts can the "writing cure" be effective? Apparently, through pencil and paper, and via cyberspace. Sheese et al. (2004) found that e-mail implementation of Pennebaker's emotional disclosure paradigm of writing about one's trauma was an effective tool for enhancing health outcomes when compared to an email-based control group. This study's findings suggested that opportunities for processing traumatic experiences could be provided to persons who would not be accessible otherwise (persons in rural areas, with little or no public/educational access to computers/internet). The idea of being able to provide therapeutic benefits via the Internet without public testimonials or traditional one-on-one psychotherapy in an office is exciting and worthy of exploration, especially in contexts where therapy is still viewed with suspicion.

Finally, our own tendency as helping professionals to subscribe to the discourse of refugee trauma may not be all that helpful. How prevalent is traumatic stress in refugees? Twenty-eight years after the war, 22 % of a sample of Greek-Cypriot refugees appeared to be suffering from traumatic stress symptoms (Agathangelou and Killian 2002). This finding is consistent with other studies of refugees and trauma survivors (Johnson and Thompson 2008; Clarke et al. 1999; Gong-Guy 1987) where 16–22 % were diagnosable with PTSD twelve to fifteen years after their displacement. Thus, as many as four out of five of survivors of traumas such as displacement and ambiguous loss do not develop traumatic stress. In addition, the relative wellness of Cypriot refugees suggests that refugees are not rife with disease and disorder, but frequently demonstrate good health outcomes (Loizos and Constantinou 2007). These findings speak to *resilience*, an alternative to the dominant discourse of traumatization. Thus, it is hoped that narratives of refugeedom and trauma can move from being a touchstone measuring our patriotism and a tool for maintaining rigid dichotomies of us and them and galvanizing ethno nationalist discourses against the Other, to becoming "weapons of mass discussion", social deliberation, and struggle that generate inclusive, contextually meaningful, and healing conversations. As helping professionals, we can facilitate clients' formation of coherent, healing narratives, while remaining conscious of the fact that members of the same family may take very different narrative paths to regain a lived synchronization with caring others, to engage no-longer ambiguous losses, to begin to mourn, and to imagine a once foreclosed future.

References

Agathangelou, A. M., & Killian, K. D. (2002). In the wake of 1974: Psychological well being and post-traumatic stress in Greek Cypriot refugee families. *Cyprus Review, 14*, 45–69.

Agathangelou, A. M., & Killian, K. D. (2009). The discourse of refugee trauma: Epistemologies of the displaced, the state, and mental health practitioners. *Cyprus Review, 21*, 19–58.

Bolton, E. E. (2000). *An exploration of the impact of self-disclosure on the development of psychological distress among Somalia peacekeepers* (Unpublished doctoral dissertation). Chapel Hill: University of North Carolina.

Boss, P. (1999). *Ambiguous loss*. Cambridge, MA: Harvard University Press.

Boss, P. (2007). Ambiguous loss theory: Challenges for scholars and practitioners. *Family Relations, 56*(2), 105–110.

Boss, P., & Carnes, D. (2012). The myth of closure. *Family Process, 51*(4), 456–469.

Chirumbolo, A., Livi, S., Mannetti, L., Pierro, A., & Kruglanski, A. (2004). Effects of need for closure on creativity in small group interactions. *European Journal of Personality, 18*(4), 265–278.

Clarke, G. N., Sack, W. H., & Goff, B. (1999). Three forms of stress in Cambodian adolescent refugees. *Journal of Abnormal Child Psychology, 21*, 65–77.

Davis, R. C., & Friedman, L. N. (1985). The emotional aftermath of crime and violence. In C. R. Figley (Ed.), *Trauma and its wake: The study and treatment of post-traumatic stress disorder* (pp. 90–112). New York, NY: Brunner/Mazel.

Figley, C. R. (1989). *Helping traumatized families*. San Francisco, CA: Jossey-Bass.

Figley, C. R. (1995). Systemic PTSD: Family treatment experiences and implications. In G. S. Everly Jr (Ed.), *Psychotraumatology: Key papers and core concepts in post-traumatic stress* (pp. 341–358). New York, NY: Plenum.

Fuchs, T. (2005). Implicit and explicit temporality. *Philosophy, Psychiatry and Philosophy, 12*(3), 195–198.

Gong-Guy, E. (1987). *The California Southeast Asian mental health needs assessment*. Oakland, CA: Asian Community Mental Health Services.

Goolishian, H. A., & Anderson, H. (1992). Strategy and intervention versus nonintervention: A matter of theory? *Journal of Marital and Family Therapy, 18*, 5–17.

Hammad, S. (2001). The missing. Retrieved from http://www.thescreamonline.com/poetry/poetry2-1/hammad/.

Johnson, H., & Thompson, A. (2008). The development and maintenance of post-traumatic stress disorder (PTSD) in civilian adult survivors of war trauma and torture: A review. *Clinical Psychology Review, 28*, 36–47.

Killian, K. D. (2015). Mission to meet our makers: A review of *Prometheus*, Part 1 [Web log comment]. Retrieved from https://www.psychologytoday.com/blog/intersections.

Loizos, P., & Constantinou, C. (2007). Hearts, as well as minds: Wellbeing and illness among Greek Cypriot refugees. *Journal of Refugee Studies, 20*(1), 86–107.

Mather, R., & Marsden, J. (2004). Trauma and temporality: On the origins of post-traumatic stress. *Theory and Psychology, 14*(2), 205–219.

Mattley, C. (2002). The temporality of emotion: Constructing past emotions. *Symbolic Interaction, 25*(3), 363–378.

McCubbin, H. I., Thompson, A. I., & McCubbin, M. A. (1996). *Family assessment: Resiliency, coping and adaptation*. Madison, WI: University of Wisconsin.

McGoldrick, M., Giordano, J., & Garcia-Preto, N. (2005). *Ethnicity and family therapy* (3rd ed.). New York, NY: Guilford.

Mead, G. H. (1932). *The philosophy of the present*. Chicago: Open Court Publishing.

Papadopoulos, R. K. (1996, Autumn). Therapeutic presence and witnessing. *The Tavistock Gazette*, 61–65.

Papadopoulos, R. K. (1998). Destructiveness, atrocities and healing: Epistemological and clinical reflections. *Journal of Analytical Psychology, 43*, 455–477.

Papadopoulos, R. K. (2001). Refugee families: Issues of systemic supervision. *Journal of Family Therapy, 23*, 405–422.

Pennebaker, J., & Seagal, J. (1999). Forming a story: The health benefits of narrative. *Journal of Clinical Psychology, 55*, 1243–1254.

Pierro, A., Kruglanski, A., & Raven, B. (2012). Motivational underpinnings of social influence in work settings: Bases of social power and the need for cognitive closure. *European Journal of Social Psychology, 42*(1), 41–52.

Ramirez-Esparza, N., & Pennebaker, J. W. (2006). Do good stories produce good health? Exploring words, language, and culture. *Narrative Inquiry, 16*(1), 211–219.

Saoulli, A. (2007, December 11). Campaign seeks to highlight sex abuse of women. Retrieved from http://www.cyprus-mail.com/news/main.php?id=36463&cat_id=1.

Sheese, B., Brown, E., & Graziano, W. (2004). Emotional expression in cyberspace: Searching for moderators of the Pennebaker disclosure effect via E-mail. *Health Psychology, 23*, 457–464.

Stolorow, R. D. (2003). Trauma and temporality. *Psychoanalytic Psychology, 20*(1), 158–161.

Thompson, E. A., McCubbin, H. I., Thompson, A. I., & Elver, K. (1995). Vulnerability and resiliency in Native Hawaiian families under stress. In H. McCubbin, E. Thompson, A. I. Thompson & J. E. Fromer (Eds.), *Resiliency in ethnic minority families: Native and immigrant American families* (Vol. 1), (pp. 115–131). Madison, WI: University of Wisconsin.

van der Veer, G. (1998). *Counselling and therapy with refugees and victims of trauma: Psychological problems of victims of war, torture and repression* (2nd ed.). New York, NY: Wiley.

Weine, S., Vojvoda, D., Hartman, S., & Hyman, L. (1997). A family survives genocide. *Psychiatry, 60*, 24–39.

Weine, S., Muzurovic, N., Kulauzovic, Y., Besic, S., Lezic, A., Mujagic, A., et al. (2004). Family consequences of refugee trauma. *Family Process, 43*, 147–160.

Yakinthou, C. (2008). The quiet deflation of den xehno? Changes in the Greek Cypriot communal narrative on the missing persons in Cyprus. *The Cyprus Review, 20*(1), 15–33.

Zetter, R. (1999). Reconceptualising the myth of return: Continuity and transition amongst the Greek-Cypriot refugees of 1974. *Journal of Refugee Studies, 12*, 1–22.

Engaging the Humanity in Front of You: Family Therapy Task Shifting in the Context of Armed Conflict

Laurie L. Charlés

Introduction

Expatriate family therapists who work as consultants outside their home countries must share their subject matter expertise in ways that are seen as useful to the people they are focused on helping (Roberts 2010). Their methods must be expansive enough to transcend traditional family therapy approaches (Morgan and Sprenkle 2007), yet remain consistent to the inherent theoretical umbrella that makes systemic family therapy unique from other disciplines. They must apply and integrate their methods in ways that respect the context of ongoing conflict (Van der Veer 1989/2003), where country dynamics are fluid and unpredictable, and when it is not always clear to determine what needs are prescient (Batniji et al. 2005). Such a complex starting point requires family therapists to look beyond issues of licensure and regulation, and consider how family therapy work is performed beyond the typical family therapy clinic (Rivett 2010).

I am a U.S. based, French speaking Latina family therapist, who has lived and worked in over half a dozen African countries since my first experience in Africa as a Peace Corps Volunteer (Togo, 99-01). I have been fortunate to work as a family therapy trainer in a number of countries in Europe and Asia, as well as in Africa. Many of the places I work are low and middle-income countries, or fragile, conflict-affected states. The definitions are important for me to understand because they set the context for the form and content of what family therapy praxis can achieve for citizens in these places. Organizations that bring me on board as a trainer to their particular project identify me as an SME—"subject matter expert"—in family therapy. I am an outsider who must immerse herself quickly, who must nimbly adapt to a fluid, dynamic setting, and, most of all, remain focused on supporting host country nationals who remain long after I am gone.

L.L. Charlés (✉)
Our Lady of the Lake University, San Antonio, TX, USA
e-mail: lcharles@ollusa.edu

One of the most useful ways outside consultants can be involved in humanitarian settings is through the delivery of supervision and clinical consultation (Patel et al. 2011). Outside subject matter experts can enhance technical capacity of host country nationals to perform family therapy methods, which increases both access and availability of psychosocial services among local people already in the field (Patel et al. 2011). I often think, no matter where I am, that my work is about issues of access to health care, including psychosocial health. I also find that my international work has greatly influenced everything I do in my professorial role in the U.S., and in ways I continue to discover.

Family Therapy Supervision

Family therapy supervision is unique from other types of clinical supervision, although in my experience it cuts across wide swathes of territory from various disciplines. What makes it more precisely unique from other kinds of clinical supervision is its particular content focus—on work that focuses "primarily with individuals, couples, families, and groups from a *systemic perspective*, one that requires expertise in *interpersonal relationships*, interaction dynamics, system theory and thinking, and *special conceptualization and procedures* that are distinct from individually oriented therapies (Bernard and Goodyear 2009, p. 5). Family therapy supervision is defined as "the process of evaluating, training, and providing oversight to trainees *using relational or systemic approaches* for the purpose of helping them attain systemic clinical skills" (p. 5).[1] The methods through which this can be done include live observation, face-to-face contact, or visual/audio technology-assisted means (Bernard and Goodyear 2009, p. 5).

In low and middle income countries and conflict-affected states, supervision occurs in the context of a lack of human resources in the mental health professions, which is a major barrier to scaling up of mental health services (Saraceno et al. 2007). For example, in my work in such settings, it has been nurses, psychiatrists, primary care physicians, or spiritual or religious healers such as imams or Buddhist priests, who deliver psychosocial support. Task shifting, which involves "delegating tasks to existing or new cadres with either less training or narrowly tailored training" (Kakuma et al. 2011), is a recommended action in countries with human resource challenges in mental health professions. More recently referred to as task-sharing (N. Ben Younis, personal communication, December, 2013), this method is critical to the delivery of family therapy clinical work in low resource

---

[1]Supervision has been defined more general as "an intervention provided by a more senior member of a profession to a more junior member or members of that same profession. The relationship is evaluative and hierarchical, extends over time, and has the simultaneous purposes of enhancing the professional functioning of the more junior person(s), monitoring the quality of professional services offered to the clients that she, he or they see, and serving as a gatekeep for those who are to enter the particular profession" (Bernard and Goodyear 2009, p. 7).

settings. It expands the above definition of family therapy supervision to focus on any non-specialized mental health and psychosocial support (MHPSS) worker.

The work presented in this chapter is from my experiences working with citizens living in the midst of an armed conflict in their country, the Central African Republic. The target population of the project in which this work took place was individuals in the family and community who were suffering from the psychosocial consequences of the conflict, including sexual and gender-based violence, injuries and trauma from forced dislocation, witnessing violence, and experiencing torture and persecution. The objective of the overall project was to provide access to free and quality psychosocial services to enhance the population's psychological state and daily functioning.

Description of the International Project

The context for the international project was a primary and secondary care hospital in a rural region of the Central African Republic.[2] The hospital, a 90-bed facility, an open-air building on a compound the size of one square kilometer, was built in the late 1950s by U.S. missionaries. Since that time, the hospital had been operating by a village committee. In 2006, an international NGO arrived, performed a needs assessment, and formed an agreement with that village committee to augment the health services that were being provided. The NGO also agreed to bring supplies and pay salaries for host country national staff.

The NGO employs 6 expatriates in the project (two nurses, an MD, a logistician, a mental health officer [me], and a project coordinator), and over 100 national staff including nurses, surgeons/physicians, mid-wives, hygienists, general health workers, a psychosocial worker, and guards. The hospital has an Inpatient department, an Outpatient clinic, a Maternity ward, a HIV/TB ward, an Emergency Room and Surgery, a section for malnourished children and their parents, and an Intensive Care suite.

The hospital is situated directly in between two areas of intense, violent conflict between rebel groups in the region. The rebel groups, non-state actors, are well-armed with RPGs, Kalishnikovs and other matériel in a lawless, rural, and somewhat neglected region of the country. Patients are often terrorized when they arrive at the hospital, as they have tried to avoid encounters with armed groups to get to us.

In the hospital, my TOR (terms of reference, or duties) as a family therapist consultant is to build on the work done by previous MHOs (Mental Health Officers), since the project began in 2007. I assist with the organization, implementation, and

---

[2]Although I have written previously on some of the experiences I had in this project (Charlés 2010), the material here is focused on supervision, and is somewhat of a "Part II," a follow up to what I wrote previously. As before, my narrative is taken from my notes from the project, and the reflexive journal that I kept while on the mission. It has not been published before.

direct provision of mental health and psychosocial support services to people in the community. My focus is on consulting with the local staff as a trainer and supervisor. What that means for me is that I do not see cases solely on my own, unless they are especially difficult or complex, or no one else is available. Rather, I see them with Victoire, the local *conseiller psychosociale*, or counselor, who has been trained and mentored by previous MHOs. She is the provider; I am the support person to her.

Context of the Family Therapy Task-Shifting and Participant Supervision

When I am working with Victoire and we are together with a client, it looks more like co-therapy or live supervision. Nearly every psychosocial consultation is conducted by Victoire, and always conducted in a local language (Sangho or Souma). Victoire then translates the session content to French for me, in real-time, as I am sitting or standing with her and the client, usually somewhere in the space of the hospital compound that might afford a bit of privacy. As the session or meeting unfolds, I offer questions or ideas, in French, and Victoire translates those back to the client, in Sangho or Souma. She does much of the questioning/joining/interviewing on her own. I act more as a co-therapist and "live" supervisor.

This collaborative, shared supervision experience as participant/observer is quite interesting as Victoire's clinical work is in the local language, I have no way to understand or translate her actual words. However, this lack of literal understanding affords me an opportunity to observe all the nuances as I witness her work firsthand, an incredibly useful advantage (Falke et al. 2015). I attend to Victoire's tone, pay close attention to her descriptions of the case (which help me understand how she conceptualizes what she is seeing), and also, watch closely the conversation between her and the patient.

When Victoire speaks in local language, I am not encumbered by literal translation in French and I find it is something of a luxury for me to just watch these non-verbal cues and listen to her. When Victoire is talking with a client, I am only two or three feet away, sitting and watching. If I have a question or query, based on something I have observed, I wait for her to finish what she says before I interrupt. If I ever think that she is talking too long or too much, I ask her to translate what the client has stated. I usually interrupt her—not the client—after the client has finished. Interestingly, in almost every way that matters, the supervision I do with Victoire is exactly like what I do in U.S., with licensed clinicians as well as graduate students. This is a surprise, a comfort, and something of a conundrum all at the same time. I had not realized how unimportant issues of translation could be.

The work is intense and engaging and I remember it in small, ordinary moments. Each day blends into the next, until the week is nothing but a blur of cases, highlighted by moments of unconventional clinical work, and also, unusual conversations I am unused to having with Victoire. Following, I present one of our shared cases, interspersing the details with my own reflections.

Case Example: Couple Session with a Woman Whose Dreams Silence Her

We had a very interesting case yesterday that is somewhat urgent, a couple, a woman with a kind of hysteria upon arrival. She seems to be traumatized, and had a vivid flashback of some kind, causing trembling, wild-eyes, difficulty speaking. Her husband is here and has been helpful. The story goes back to displacement from the village due to killing. They have lived in the bush now, for three months.
3 p.m. M. Hospital, Central African Republic

I just came from a 45 min session with a woman, Safiatou, who arrived at the hospital early this a.m. with her husband. Safiatou is 4 months pregnant with her 7th child. She knows the hospital as she is being followed in the outpatient clinic for pre-natal care. Right before lunch one of the physicians radio'd me (we use high frequency radios to communicate with each other in the hospital compound) to request a consult as the woman was diagnosed upon arrival with "l'hysterie." Nursing staff described her as trembling, as noticeably calmer when her husband left the room, and with a "bewildered" look on her face.

I agree to see her after lunch, and tried to think about who I could ask to help me translate, as Victoire is out sick today. I cannot do any sessions in French here because the hospital patients do not speak French. However, the all the staff speak French, and in addition, they also speak one or both of the local languages, Sangho and Souma. We are accustomed to working in three languages here; my project team works in English and French, the team of host country nationals in Sangho or Souma and French, and the clients, Sangho or Souma. Often it takes several languages to accomplish a session.

As so many emergency or unexpected cases arise in the hospital, I have been trying to focus on the staff with have had a bit of training in basic counselling skills. Their narrow training in psychosocial skills combined with their excellent proficiency as medical providers make a perfect opportunity for task-shifting. Using the skill mix of non-specialized health care providers to delivery MHPSS services is critical in countries like CAR, with minimal human resource capacity in mental health, and is particularly so during a humanitarian context, when resources tend to be scarce anyway.

One sure bet for me when Victoire is not available is always the maternity staff. They have had a few basic trainings in counselling, so they are perfect candidates for task-sharing. Our MHPSS caseload is an opportunity for them to augment their skill set with family therapy methods. Task-shifting with other staff means more choices and better coverage of services for the patients.

I walk in the intense plus 40° heat to maternity to see what I can do. In the heat my face is burning. I splash cold water on my face after lunch and put on more sunscreen but in this heat, it still feels like my face is on fire. I don't want to bother with my hat. It's just too hot for a hat even. I can feel the skin reddening on the back of my neck.

Inside maternity, the first person I see is Marina, the supervisor. I really should ask permission, from her, to use one of her staff this way. So I take a minute to question her (after she suggests I shut the door) about the woman and my request. Marina says she will see if the woman is there, and also, what language she speaks, Sangho or Souma. That will also tell us who might be the staff to ask to translate.

Marina walks out of the room and I sweat and drip, wondering how it is Marina can appear so fresh and dry. She comes back in and tells me Brigit can work with me, and then: "*Bonne Collaboration!*" and at the last minute I ask her if she thinks it is a good idea or not that I work with one of the matrons? Since the woman is a patient here in maternity and will see this matron often and maybe it will be confusing? I am thinking about our professional codes of ethics that talk about dual relationships. It's not that the principle doesn't make sense here, but in a low-resource setting, the choices we have limit our ability to exclude others. Marina says she understands. But what to do? Maybe it's not a problem? I really need to have some flexibility here; I can't put unnecessary restrictions on anything; I need to have the possibility to work with anyone who is available. So, I tell Marina that I will use Brigit and explain to mother that this is a translation and maybe it will be another person next time and that Brigit is helping me. Marina agrees.

We enter the room. It's a large room with 4 or 5 beds, but only one patient in one bed. It is Safiatou, lying down, and looking quite small and weak. I take a seat on the bed opposite her and Brigit I think is asking her to sit up. She has a wild look in her eyes. Her face is tight, and her braids fuzzy, closely matted to her head. She looks in her 20's, not too young, not too old, but if she looks like anything, she looks afraid. Her eyes are wide and when I talk she looks at me and watches my face. Her arms and legs are small and if you look at her quickly, you may not notice that she is 4 months pregnant. She is thin, in a way that is not healthy looking, but rather, suggests frailty. And where to start? What question first?

I explain first who I am—an expat, I work here in the hospital, with the medical team. I have a colleague, Victoire, who is sick today, otherwise it would be her talking to you. I invited my friend Birgit so that she could translate for me. Is that okay with you?

She accepts. I ask Birgit to explain that what we talk about is confidential, we won't tell people outside the medical team, or people in the village, or even her husband, sitting outside the room. At a certain point in the translation, I see Safiatou's head nod, up and down, quietly.

Then I ask if Birgit could find out something about her life, who does she live with, where is her home?

> I live in Zemio, I have 6 children and 7th is on the way. I was born in Bossangoua, but moved to Zemio because that is where my husband is from.

> What brought you here today? How do you feel right now?

> I started having pains in my head, my stomach, since yesterday. I am having trouble expressing myself; I am having problems "à parler." (As she talks, her eyes grow wider and her facial movements become slightly jerky. Her eyes seem to be seeking something out, inspecting vividly, wherever she directs her gaze when she is talking. She has the same look when she is listening, but the jerking is much less. The wild, wide eyes face you but the jerking stops).

> Can you describe how you feel right now?

Safiatou answers me without hesitation. "I feel fine. But my husband brought me this morning because I was not feeling good. Thank you for speaking to me, I came here because I did not feel good and now you are talking and listening to me and thank you I thank you." (When Brigit translates this, I ask her to translate back my own thanks to Safiatou for talking as she didn't have to talk and she did talk and is talking so thank you).

> I ask, "Are you afraid of something?"
> She says she is afraid of nothing right now.

If I were to be seeing this case with my family therapy trainees at our clinic in the U.S., we would be focusing intently on the crisis nature of her presentation, and perhaps possible hospitalization, recommending a full medical and perhaps even a psychiatric assessment. But here, I am in a hospital already. In fact, I am perhaps in the only nearby place for people to come for psychosocial support. It is also a "safe" place, even in the midst of this armed conflict; as an MSF hospital, it is accepted by the community—both soldiers/rebels and non-combatants—as a no-weapons zone that is respected as a neutral space. So, what to do? Essentially, we must do the examination, in two languages, while task-shifting and translating at the same time. So: I follow the woman's expressions and words closely, as well as the relationship I am developing in situ with my translator Brigit. She becomes part of the client system with me.

Then an important detail comes out. Safiatou states: *"Three months ago, the army came to our village. They took the village. Since then, we have been living in the bush. Until two days ago, when husband brought me out because I was not feeling well. My mother in law also lives with us. She is not well. I have a problem speaking. Maybe you should talk to my husband to help because I have a problem speaking."*

The symptoms started 4 days ago.

Safiatou continues: "My mother-in-law stopped talking to me 5 days ago. I cook the food; she doesn't take it. I don't know why she stopped talking to me. She is not well."

Then she adds, *"Maybe it is sorcerie that has caused my maladie."*

At this translation, Birgit breaks the barrier as a translator. She smiles she giggles, she laughs, she chuckles at the client's words. I remember in that moment that although both women are from CAR, both are speaking Souma, the client and the nurse might as well be from different countries. Their identities in that moment are quite far apart, despite their common nationality and language, and I see that in this moment, I am more aligned with the client than Birgit is. Birgit is from the city, but Safiatou is clearly not. City dwellers in CAR do not express such open beliefs in sorcery. Safiatou adds one more thought: "My mother in law started speaking to me one day ago. Now I don't know how I should express myself."

Thus, Safiatou's presentation at the hospital. The medical officer confirms: There is nothing physically wrong with her.

We bring in the husband into the session. The situation with Safiatou is a mystery, and I am not sure how much the husband is aware or part of his wife's problem. What role does he play? This is not unusual to consider how another family member is engaged in the client's presenting issues, but it's the first time I've had a situation like this in another language, in the middle of a conflict zone, where, as I've learned over the months, sorcery is one of the worst things you can say is happening to you. A number of patients have entered the hospital after being identified as sorcerers, and then tortured by a faction in the community.

The husband enters the room with Brigit. Can you explain that we talked to her and she suggested we talk to him? I ask Brigit. I explain: "We work here in the hospital together to help the people admitted or who come here for treatment. Can he tell us in his opinion what happened when his wife first became sick?" The husband recounts in great detail the dream.

What does he see that tells him his wife is so ill? (Trembling, difficulty speaking)
How does he think his wife is doing right now? (a little better)
How does she seem better? (she is not trembling)
How did he decide to bring her to the hospital? (I knew if she was sick I should bring her. It's my first reaction. I am concerned about her health. God will make things better. I know here she can get treatment, she can get help, there are doctors, there are nurses, she can get help here.)

I ask for a detail somewhere in here about the moment he decided he must do something. In family therapy work, it is a long-standing hallmark to focus on the presenting concerns of the client, in preference to asking about past history or childhood experience. In situations like this one in CAR, where communities are encountering many problems inherent to a humanitarian situation, alongside their significant historical origins and contextual subtleties, I focus yet more micro-attention on the present. What is the precipitating event that brought Safiatou to the hospital? What was the key moment that shifted the client's view to come to us?

The husband has a ready answer for me. He recounts a dream that happened Sunday before last. He was at the farm and when he returned home early in the a. m., his wife Safiatou told him about it; the next day, that dream came true. This made Safiatou very frightened. Safiatou had another dream a few days later and he heard her scream, "*Ne me tuer pas! Ne me tuer pas!*" Writhing and crying out, Safiatou told her husband that in her dream she was shot in her inside left knee, and in the back of her neck, at the base of her head. Since then she has been deathly afraid that this dream also will come true. And at 1 a.m. yesterday morning, Wednesday a.m. very early, she had the trembling and at that moment he decided to bring her to the hospital.

Throughout my interview with the husband, Safiatou is extremely calm, quiet, and placid. She sits upright, gracefully even, as he talks. She is looking straight ahead, not at me or Birgit or anyone. When I talk to her, she makes eye contact. I ask her if she have anything to add to what her husband has said? To that, she says no.

At the end, I ask, what would she like to see change? The thing she would like to most improve? She states she would like to be better so she can continue to look after her children. She prays to God that she will be better. I ask how long they've been married (Since 1994). She is 29 years old.

We do a brief mental status exam. She is oriented times three. I ask her What are the names of your children? Where are we? What is the date today? (Six children, we are in the region hospital, it is Wednesday—bad translation for names of children and Birgit gives me numbers instead).

I try to find out the history of coming to the hospital, and also, where they lived and where they live now, and why they moved. What is their situation now? And this is where things begin to make sense. Among other circumstances, multiple displacements are common in countries in the midst of ongoing conflict (Phama et al. 2010). In Safiatou's case, the most recent displacement resulted in a particularly horrible event: Their home was destroyed.

> We moved after military came to Boria three months ago, a General came through and scared everyone by staging an offensive. All fled to the bush. We live in the bush and have for three months. We are lucky because we have managed to farm there, peanuts, corn, manioc. Our home in Boria is gone, only one wall remains.

I try to find out more specifically what happened in Boria three months ago. What did they see? Witness? Hear about? Experience? I can only find out the name of the general, and that he started an offensive. I am not sure where she/he was at that moment, what time of day it was, what she might have seen, did she join them all together, was she alone, try to determine if it is possible that there was something she could have experienced that her husband would know nothing about. But I can't get there between the French-Souma translation and the reporting difficulty and the newness of my relationship with the translator Birgit.

> I leave it. I don't need to know all the details of the traumatic event in order to be helpful (Papadopolous 2005). Instead, I compliment the husband on bringing his wife. I tell him, "We will work hard to try to figure out a solution for her. We are glad you are here—that helps very much."

My observations are that he is an excellent, detailed reporter, and in fact contrary to what I thought she appears much calmer with him present. It's as if she can relax with him telling the story; she doesn't have to do it. Her demeanor changed completely. He fills out the details of the skeletal version she told us. He is talkative, interested, polite but not overly so, and appears concerned. Her eyes only get a bit wild now and again during this hour long session.

Birgit does an excellent job translating and it is a pleasure to work with her. She is sensitive, patient, she stops and starts in short phrases, bite-size pieces that are easy to follow. She is good at taking direction: Can you find out…. I want to know….. Let's ask if….. and even when I talk to the clients directly she handles it: "We are glad you are here for your wife …." In situations like this one, where there are three or four languages between client/clinician/translator, it is inefficient to focus on perfect literal translation. Rather, the focus is on the relationships—between the actors, myself and Birgit included—and also, how closely approximate we can get to the client's understanding of her experience.

This understanding is not conveyed only by language—not by words, nor phrases. As in all systemic family therapy, the meta-communication, the non-verbal process, is most beneficial to contextualizing the content. It is particularly so for me working in CAR. English, French, Sangho, Souma: bits and pieces of these tell me the content I need to know, certainly. But it is the client's demeanor, alone, with her husband, and during the telling and retelling of her story that to me has been most beneficial to my conceptualization of her situation. In fact, I often wonder if a focus too much on literal, correct language translation is a hindrance at times, rather than an asset.

The next morning Victoire accompanies me to meet Safiatou. Victoire actually knows her (it's a small area and hard not to know someone); their parents know each other. Safiatou looks completely different: calm, talkative, and at ease. She has a baby with her, and her mother in law. Safiatou states she had slept well even though she did not have any medicine to help her sleep. When asked how this could have happened, one of the solution-focused questions that work so well in this setting, the woman says it is because of God. God helped her; she knew it had to be God because there was no medication given. We assured Safiatou she could return anytime to the hospital, bad dreams or not.

A few days later, we see Safiatou again, because she arrives in the hospital only a few days after she's been discharged. Why? Her child is sick. Victoire fills me in on the child's health and then suggests we go visit Safiatou in pediatric ward. Safiatou looks wonderful. Completely recovered.

We agree to do a consultation but only because we've promised Safiatou that it will only consist of 1 question. She agrees and follows us to extra *soin intensif* room. As I always have my training hat on with my clinician one, I ask Victoire if she can guess the question? The type of intense, in-the-moment participant-supervision we are doing is also an opportunity to model interventions and provide subtle feedback and assistance (Falke et al. 2015). Victoire and I have built a strong relationship together; I trust her clinical judgment. I have also been humbled by her thoughtful, interesting and open queries about clinical work.

Victoire says we can ask, "Perhaps if she's had more nightmares?" and I say, "Yes that's the idea….but let's ask her *how in hindsight she was able to overcome this problem?* Victoire nods, understanding my intention to ask about the client's resources. She asks Safiatou, who responds: "It was God's program. If he would have wanted me to die, I would have died."

Discussion: From What is Possible to What is Sustainable

Before I arrived in CAR, I had my doubts about what actually would be possible in terms of fulfilling mental health needs, and the utility of providing something as abstract and intangible as "mental health" care. The project in CAR took place what feels like a lifetime ago. Since then, my work has taken me to other places where ongoing, armed conflict is happening at the same time as psychosocial support (and family therapy training and service delivery). So. My questions now are not about if it's possible, but rather, *what* is possible? And, more specifically, what is *sustainable*?

First, I agree that task-sharing, especially on complex cases (such as families or couples' methods, which may be very new for psychosocial workers) is critical. The skill mix set that task-sharing supports, if enhanced by outside consultants, can have long-lasting effects on trainees, their supervisees, and the clients they see. For instance, some of the psychiatrists I have worked with in areas of armed conflict—who had very little traditional training in psychotherapy interventions—have learned to implement, and then master, as well as train others to implement and master, such complex interventions as using four-generation genograms specific to the context of armed conflict. These are things my own students in the U.S. have trouble doing after two years of study, and which I still cannot do nearly as well after 15 years of practice.

Another response that works incredibly well, as a sustainability measure as well as a supervisory one, is to involve and include interdisciplinary teams in every step of training. Diverse teams (in terms of their professional training) mean broader sets of skills can be brought to bear when a family is seeking assistance. First-responders or front-line people in the humanitarian situation (whomever they may be) are critical to focus on for this reason: where is access to services happening in the humanitarian situation? Is the project targeting those communities for training and supervision? This is standard practice in international humanitarian settings where MHPSS projects take place. Yet, it is critical for me to be certain that I also understand what this looks like on the ground, as there is often a significant gap between what the needs are in the field and what actually happens in the design of a project (Tol et al. 2011).

Third, in terms of family therapy, content knowledge must be crystallized in way that serves practice in the setting. In humanitarian settings, the pace of MHPSS service delivery is often urgent. The pace is set by the country dynamics, and those contextual factors in a place shape the therapy content (for example, discussing the implications of being targeted as a sorcerer, rather than another intersectional identity that we might see in western contexts); however, we must still attend to client's theory of change, ask about and incorporate their belief systems into our interventions, and highlight strengths every place we can. Doing this competently requires more than theoretical skill; it requires critical attention to local knowledge.

It is a hallmark of the field to apply in practice the key idea that each family has its own worldview, which must be taken into account if one is to promote meaningful change. In my experience, this does not change in humanitarian settings; rather, what changes most is the external setting—lack of resources we are accustomed to in non-humanitarian settings such as electricity, potable drinking water, functional institutions, rule of law. These indicators deftly influence the type of problems families face, and the challenges communities have to thrive.

References

Batniji, R., van Ommeren, M., & Saraceno, B. (2005). Mental and social health in disasters: Relating qualitative social science research and the Sphere standard. *Social Science and Medicine, 62*, 1853–1864.

Bernard, J., & Goodyear, R. (2009). *Fundamentals of clinical supervision.* New York, NY: Pearson.

Charlés, L. L. (2010). Family therapists as front line mental health providers in war-affected regions: Using reflecting teams, scaling questions, and family members in a hospital in Central Africa. *Journal of Family Therapy, 32*, 27–42.

Falke, S. I., Lawson, L., Pandit, M. L., & Patrick, E. A. (2015). Participant supervision: Supervisor and supervisee experiences of cotherapy. *Journal of Marital and Family Therapy, 41*, 150–162. doi:10.1111/jmft.12039.

Kakuma, R., Minas, H., Ginneken, N., Dal Poz, M. R., Desiraju, K., Morris, J., & Scheffler, R. M. (2011). Human resources for mental health care: Current situation and strategies for action. *Lancet, 378*, 1654–1663.

Morgan, M., & Sprenkle, D. (2007). Toward a common-factors approach to supervision. *Journal of Marital and Family Therapy, 33*, 1–17.

Papadopoulos, R. K. (2005). 'But how can I help if I don't know?' Supervising work with refugee families. In. D. Campbell & B. Mason (Eds.), *Perspectives on Supervision* (pp. 157–180). London, England: Karnac.

Patel, V., Chowdhary, N., Rahman, A., & Verdeli, H. (2011). Improving access to psychological treatments: Lessons from developing countries. *Behavior Research and Therapy, 49*, 523–528.

Phama, P. N., Vincka, P., & Weinstein, H. M. (2010). Human rights, transitional justice, public health and social reconstruction. *Social Science and Medicine, 70*, 98–105.

Rivett, M. (2010). Looking beyond the clinic. *Journal of Family Therapy, 32*, 1–3.

Roberts, J. (2010). Teaching and learning with therapists who work with street children and their families. *Family Process, 9*(3), 385–404.

Saraceno, B., van Ommeren, M., Batniji, R., Cohen, A., Gureje, O., Mahoney, J., & Underhill, C. (2007). Barriers to improvement of mental health services in low-income and middle-income countries. *Lancet, 370*, 1164–1174. doi:10.1016/S0140-6736(07)61263-X.

Tol, W. A., Patel, V., Tomlinson, M., Baingana, F., Galappatti, A., Panter-Brick, C., & van Ommeren, M. (2011). Research priorities for mental health and psychosocial support in humanitarian settings. *PLoS Medicine, 8*(9), e1001096. doi:10.1371/journal.pmed.1001096.

Van der Veer, G. (1989/2003). *Training counselors in areas of armed conflict within a community approach.* Utrecht, Netherlands: Pharos.

Family Therapy in Libya: Navigating Uncharted Waters

Malak Ben Giaber

Introduction

Reaching Back to Move Forward…

When I was asked to write this chapter, I initially felt it would not be possible. It was during the winter months of 2014 , when I was displaced to Guildford, England. I would have to reflect on my personal and professional journey since I had taken part in the training on psychological intervention in post-conflict Libya. I was apprehensive about my ability to do that. The training of almost two years prior seemed to belong to the distant past. So much has happened since the training stopped and as warring militias tore my country, Libya, apart. My family, my husband and three children had to leave home one night in July 2014. It was safer to move into the center of Tripoli than to stay in the outskirts where the fighting was more intense. We were fortunate to be able to move into my father's house, which was fully furnished and comfortable. We only left with backpacks that night; my 16-year-old daughter was happy she could take along her guitar and we had a few items of clothing each. There was a washer and dryer so we would be fine for a couple of days until things settled and we could return home.

We have not been back since, except for the occasional short visit or to get some photographs and books. The situation is calmer, at a stalemate but we have moved on as a family. I had continued to work that summer, until the end of September, at a mental health clinic and helped set up a psychosocial support team, which reached

---

Independent Practitioner.

M.B. Giaber (✉)
Tripoli, Libya

© American Family Therapy Academy 2016
L.L. Charlés and G. Samarasinghe (eds.), *Family Therapy in Global Humanitarian Contexts*, AFTA SpringerBriefs in Family Therapy,
DOI 10.1007/978-3-319-39271-4_9

out to internally displaced persons (IDPs)[1] coming to Tripoli from nearby towns affected by the fighting. I stayed in Tripoli while my family moved to the UK where the children could continue their education and get on with their lives in safer conditions. I did not want to leave as there was so much to do and I felt there was a need for my services at both the clinic and working with the team. However, eventually I had to face the reality that I had a three-year-old son, a pubescent, 12 year old daughter who did not want to leave her school and friends in Libya and continuously reminded us what horrible parents we were to bring her to England against her will.

I was torn about leaving but it had to be. I told a friend that my children will never forgive me for this. I will be to blame when 20 years from now my daughter will be sitting in a therapy session struggling with abandonment issues because her mum chose her work over the family. My friend lightheartedly responded that as a mother, I am responsible for everything that goes wrong anyway. Having joined the family in the UK, I fell into utter emptiness. I felt inadequate not being able to be there for my children as I was self-absorbed with my predicament, constantly thinking of the clients I had abandoned, the fate of my country and how life looked so bleak. I referred to us, my family and myself, as the "displaced well or well displaced" as I was very aware of how fortunate we were to have the luxury of choosing where we would be "displaced". I worked with people who simply did not have that option. What I found the most distressing and the most shared difficulty with IDPs I have met since, was accepting the fact that you can forcefully be removed and put somewhere else. It was that disheartening feeling of disempowerment, a feeling of complete submissiveness; similar to what a victim of abuse does for self-preservation—a type of shame that comes with having to be submissive for the sake of survival.

It was at this point that I was asked to write this chapter. It took a lot of effort to think back on the training that started in May 2013, the events and what it was like during that time. I had forgotten that all I did as a professional up to that point was directly related to experiences I had and the skills learned in the WHO psychotherapeutic interventions training course. I started to reach back to the events of the last two years, to find my bearings. Clearly, the training gave me the tools to cope with the challenges of a displaced person; not only personally, but also in the scope of providing support to others.

In the summer of 2014, when Tripoli started hurting, when the noise of constant bombing no longer startled us, when the psychosocial support team was visibly showing signs of exhaustion, I decided to hold weekly group meetings, where the team would meet to discuss issues and difficulties they encountered in their work.

---

[1] The IOM defines IDPs as: "….among the most vulnerable people in the world today. Forced to leave their homes as a result of armed conflict, gross violations of human rights and other traumatic events, once displaced they nearly always continue to suffer from conditions of insecurity, severe deprivation and discrimination. ….[R]esponsibility for addressing the plight of internally displaced lies first and foremost with the State concerned, which more often than not proves unable or unwilling to do so, thereby raisingthe need for outside concern and involvement."

All the elements of the training came to life. A member of the team, the mother of a martyr of the revolution, was exhaustedly recounting how she could not handle this current war: each of her remaining two sons supported opposing factions. She said she would come home from working with IDPs only to find her sons arguing their respective positions. She tearfully shared that she could deal with her son's death, but to have this ongoing fighting at home, a continuation of the fighting outside, was more than she could endure. This was three months after the training stopped. Little did I expect that I would be living through the role-play scenarios. I joked to myself that I got the point; was this a test? Could I not demonstrate that I would know what to do 'in real life' without such radical means of testing?

The fact that I could recall these experiences and I was still able to put them into context was an indicator that I might be able to write this chapter after all. Dr. Laurie Charlés, encouraged me in a casual way that I could still get something out of this. The training and humanitarian work in the Libyan context seemed far from my current reality but it was within reach and it was so worthy of retrospection. This might have been my first encounter with "contextual truth," which invariably made me relate to myself and everything else from a systemic perspective (Bateson 1972; von Bertalanffy 1968). It all gradually came together.

Spring: The Time to Deliver…

[handwritten margin note: Rebuilding the country after the fall of a regime can take generations! & people do not expect this]

In the spring of 2013, the war had been over for one and a half years. The revolution was done, Gadhaffi was gone and we Libyans were full of hope in wanting to get Libya back on her feet again. Like many Libyans, I was optimistic in my efforts to help in rebuilding the country. I belong to a large group of Libyans who fully supported the 17th of February Revolution, though I did not actively take part in the war to end Gadhaffi's regime. I felt now was the time to participate, to give where I could, to deliver on those unspoken promises I made to myself during the summer of 2011 when it looked like this war would never end. It did. It ended in August 2011. It seemed like Libyans were out of breath and somewhat drained by the experience but the exhilaration of knowing the worst was over and only better things are yet to come helped us regenerate our efforts. We had overcome the hurdles; we could see the finish line and thought all we had to do was move forward. To me the finish line was a settled Libya; a Libya at peace with herself, where democracy would put things into place and ensure good governance, the infrastructure would gradually be rebuilt, and we were all there to guide Libya through this process.

By the spring of 2013, it had taken me over a year to find my bearings, to make sense of my place in the new Libya, to fully process what had happened and to start my engagement as a citizen. At the age of 40, I had never known that phenomenon.

To feel as an active part of a system, to have a sense of civic duty towards this system and to understand and appreciate my responsibility towards others in my community was a sobering and yet challenging shift. It was a novel experience and one that I gradually realized, was laced with idealism and naiveté. It turned out that the finish line was elusive and that we could not possibly deal with the aftermath of a war without the aid, in the form of knowledge and expertise, of the international community.

Can I Deliver?

I was in the middle of an online Master's degree in counseling psychology. Many were approaching me about starting to offer my services and I was reluctant due to the ethical considerations concerning my competence, not having received the adequate applied skills, training and supervision. I felt there was a huge gap between course work, analyzing research articles and actually applying this knowledge as a practitioner. I was struggling to find a way to practice what I was learning but there was no framework within which this could be applied. At the time, I was desperately trying to find a local association or group in the helping professions that I could refer to in establishing the necessary ethical guidelines to practice. There was none to be found. In Tripoli, there were about ten psychiatrists whose only engagement with therapists or counselors was in the scope of administering IQ tests. Therefore, when an ex-colleague, a social worker at the El-Razi Hospital for Mental Health in Tripoli, whom I had known since I did an internship in the hospital years prior, contacted me about the WHO and the Ministry of Health training in Psychological Interventions, I was more than ready.

An Opportunity Comes Knocking

I was curious and intrigued. As with many endeavors in Libya, the training program seemed vague. The location, the number of trainees and their background as well as the actual trainers and the specifics of the skills we would be trained in, all seemed to change each day leading up to the beginning of the training in the last week of May 2013. However, that all did not matter. It was an opportunity and we were flexible enough to take the uncertainty in our stride. This uncertainty was something we discussed openly, that we would be on standby, ready to start as soon as everything was arranged. However, what I did not discuss openly was my questioning why we were offered this opportunity. Having grown up in Libya under the Gadhaffi regime it seemed second nature to distrust and to question the motives behind actions. Why would the WHO be offering this training to us Libyans? What were this organization's motives? We had never been exposed to humanitarian work before. As far as I was concerned, humanitarian interventions were what organizations with awe-inspiring names did in times of famine or epidemics. I found out later when the training started that fellow trainees had the same doubts. However, they took them further, with twists that are more imaginative; one trainer was thought a spy while the other must have been an undercover missionary.

The phrase that was gaining popularity in Libya in those days was "hidden agenda" and it was commonly used to describe just about any activity one could not make sense of in an unfamiliar and constantly changing environment. By the time these doubts were voiced amongst the trainees, providing fodder for coffee-break chatter, I had no interest in exploring them further. I had become fascinated with the material and was soaking up like a sponge what the first trainer from Belgium was teaching us on psychological first aid (PFA). I found that establishing whether there was a hidden agenda was inconsequential, as I was sold on this training by the time the second trainer, Dr. Laurie Charlés, arrived in Tripoli to introduce us to family therapy (FT).

Family Therapy…Really? Now? Here?

We had just completed the first module, PFA, which helped to put things into perspective. However, when we were told that the next training topic would be Family Therapy, I just could not make sense of it. How did that fit into humanitarian work? Was that not the new approach used especially in the United States, targeting families that were falling apart? How would that fit into Libyan society, which is very proud of the family institution, no matter how flawed it may be? How would family members come together with a complete stranger to work out issues that are highly sensitive and private? I could not imagine such a scene: a constellation of (for instance) parents, teenage girls, and their older brothers, all trying to communicate and interact in this type of context. I wondered how I would react to Family Therapy, a course I had always avoided during my master's studies. I questioned whether it was really what we needed in this type of training and whether it would "sit well" in a cultural sense. Unbeknownst to me, in the lead up to this training, preparing to accept and assimilate, I was preoccupied with the social stage (Haley and Richeport-Haley 2007). It is very likely that our trainer was doing the same…

It all started to make sense with the mention of violence, trauma and war. Things started to become more lucid. Suddenly connections between elements of the events started to appear. What we have been through as a nation and how that reflected on us as individuals, and how we perceived ourselves within this system; these factors started defining who we were and what we were doing. It became clear that my view of family therapy would change. I couldn't possibly be in this field, training to be a psychotherapist, thinking about helping people, without taking into consideration the relationships and the sense of family and community within which we exist. Through family therapy I have come to view the family in a completely different light. I have come to realize that the family unit can be the source of trouble and distress, yet we do not give up on it that easily. The unit can be as flawed and as weak as an ailing body yet there seems to be this innate need to want to keep it going. We strive to understand connections, we hope to make changes and find solutions. FT provides us with the tools to understand, put into perspective and accept the limitations of this unit. By doing so we re-evaluate our positions in the system and this in turn allows us to shift and become more flexible in our outlooks and expectations. This understanding of the system encourages hope and optimism, which we see in the resilience as well as the ability of clients to find solutions to their difficulties once they are guided to trust themselves with exploring the alternatives (Franklin et al. 2012).

This new outlook on FT also influenced my ideas about my own family. How I was raised, by whom, and where this happened. This new way of thinking continues to remind me just how embedded we are in the systems we exist in. I cannot loosen the ties I have with my family of origin, my parents, my upbringing; nor can I shake off my adolescent daughter who has ability to frustrate the living daylights out of me. Similarly, I would find it equally difficult to dissociate who I am from Libya. I am very aware of the difficulty of making such a statement; I could have been spared this type of view of myself and the world, yet my exposure to FT now makes that attempt rather futile. Moreover, with the realization that change and development can really only be viewed and understood in the context of a system, I no longer want to spare myself that challenge.

When I explore the relationships between my clients' family members, I attain a deeper understanding of the dynamics, the entanglements, and the issues that need tackling. Furthermore, I have found myself applying the same strategy in facing my own struggles, reaching further out or deeper down to understand my position and how I relate to my reality. If this training had been offered anywhere else, I would expect it to have been a different experience. If the WHO in Cairo for instance, was providing this type of applied skills training in psychological interventions to future professionals, and I happened to be attending on the grounds of being a professional in this field from neighboring Libya, I still think my experience would have been different. The context made all the difference. We were involved with psychological interventions with families, families that were affected by the war, and as it turns out not in "post conflict" Libya but rather in a system of ongoing internal struggle similar to what we see in cyclical patterns within families. It was almost serendipitous, when we watched in disbelief how things started to unravel towards the end of the training, abruptly and prematurely ending it in July 2014, relegating its application to the future as a preventative measure, rather than an intervention as was originally intended.

This type of training was a first in my experience. Its focus on applied, practical and immediately deliverable services was of great value. At the time, I was working at a mental health clinic in Tripoli, as part of a team of psychiatrists, psychologists and social workers, providing psycho-education and counseling to patients referred by my colleagues. Three times a week I was able to go straight from the training to the clinic enabled with the tools to help me be a better counsellor. I had previously avoided thinking of the client's family. It was too much to handle I thought. Besides, it was hard enough trying to figure out one person's difficulties leave alone a group of individuals constituting a family. The task seemed daunting.

Role Plays: As Real as It Gets

Family therapy changed the way I perceived systems and relationships and also, encouraged me to step outside my comfort zone, immersing myself in a new reality with new constellations of interactions, where I had to engage with everyone involved in a constructive manner. This became apparent through the role-plays that were used in the family therapy training. I was apprehensive about these. Insecure in my acting skills, and not confident enough to reveal my professional limitations in front of fellow trainees, I questioned the benefit we would get out of these. Little did I know that every single scenario carried within it all the intricacies of family dynamics. Every scenario offered the toolbox of countless possibilities and approaches I could use as a practitioner. Stories unfolded within the context of a role-play. As we watched or participated, we were allowed a bird's eye view of the situation we were in and how specific historical events had affected us. It seemed like we were not aware of our reality. Being in a specific situation, for example living in the aftermath of war, going through the labor and teething pains of a new political reality, is not something we were consciously experiencing. As far as I was concerned, we were going through the motions and reacting the best we could to the forces that be but it almost felt like things were moving too fast so there was no point keeping up. Role-plays on the other hand, made me stop and think. How did this war affect the participants in the role-play? How did it affect the characters they had adopted for those 10 min? What went wrong? What went right? Who is doing what, where and when? As these questions went through my head, I inevitably directed them towards myself. How did this war affect me? How did loss affect my loved ones? What is working? What is not? How are we coping? It turned out that role plays not only addressed emotional issues we were not conscious of, but they also served as an example of how fundamental assumptions such as homeostasis and negative or positive feedback can guide our work with families (Bateson 1972).

I could not fathom engaging in this thought process simply by following textbook instructions or even by being told by a seasoned professional that this is what I needed to do. After the first role-plays ended, it was almost like a cathartic experience. There were those moments of shared recognition when very little needed to be said to communicate that we understood each other. Suddenly we felt comfortable using words such as trauma, violence, pain and suffering. Role-plays validated and legitimized what we felt but were uneasy about expressing. We could not show that we were weak. That we weren't up to the responsibility of a revolution, that the civil war did actually bring out the worst in us, that we were not as strong and united as we believed ourselves to be and that we were a disappointment to ourselves. Lastly, and the most burdensome of all, we had let down all those who lost their lives fighting for what we believed in.

In this sense, the training, and the role-plays in particular, provided the stage to express, communicate and reveal our deepest fears in a protected and nourishing environment. I thought it ingenious that we would learn about ourselves while we were being taught about how to help others. It worked so well, it was like magic. Perhaps that is what proper learning was all about; I had grown up in a dictatorship where critical thinking was nonexistent, and rote learning was the educational method of choice. Having completed my secondary education in Europe and then receiving my BA in Canada, I had to learn to think about learning in a different way.

However, this experience was not the kind of learning that was generalizable to the Libyan context. Once back there, even as a 40 year old, in the context of a training, I found myself not able to argue or engage in critical thinking without feeling threatened or doomed to fail. Arguing with my fellow trainees, that homosexuality was not deviant behavior, to be punished by beating with an iron rod, set me up for failure. I decided then that it was all right to feel confused and inadequate but to walk away as a failure would add insult to injury. At this point, I realized that the mere fact that I could express a different perspective on homosexuality was good enough. It did not have to go anywhere; it could just land in the middle of that discussion circle with a flop. A flop was a good place to start. After all, working in this field was all about acceptance, so I would have to accept that others hold opinions and views that run counter to my own and I would still need to find a workable common ground no matter how different or opposing those views are. It was only later that I appreciated the training had provided us with an opportunity to become aware of our limitations, accept our differences and allow for the novelty of corrective experiences.

Family Therapy and Politics: Part and Parcel

It was fascinating to see that what happened during the training was a reflection of the discourse and quality of interaction occurring outside in our everyday lives. Ever since things started to take a turn for the worse in the summer of 2014, I watch the events unfold and often wonder how well served politicians would be if they were taught to apply the interactive skills used in FT. I try to imagine how concepts like joining, pacing and reflecting (Charlés, personal communication 2013) would make politics so much more palatable, where opposing parties can learn to listen, accept and validate one another. I have always tried to avoid politics, often using the cliché that it is a dirty game and have often questioned the motives of politicians. Therefore, I found it rather unsettling when I became more concerned with the day-to-day politics that affected our lives. It was a love hate relationship; I loved to hate our politics and could not resist keeping away. I made dear friends who were very involved with the political scene and many were political activists who abandoned the comfort of secure jobs and life in the western world to come to Libya to help unconditionally. I am still trying to reconcile with concepts like identity, belonging and civic duty; I am hoping that this reconciliatory process will eventually help accommodate both my psychological and my political sense of self.

Family politics: A Case in Point I always thought that I could keep politics out of my profession, believing that the therapeutic relationship could be kept untarnished by such influences. I was in for a big surprise. This became clear when the first family I worked with was comprised of a divorced mother (my client) her rebel teenage daughter, four uncles who ranged from the radically religious to the conservative-traditional to the business-minded moderate, three unmarried aunts and the grandmother–all living in the same house.

Each member of this family wanted to have their way, wanting to "guide and help" their divorced sister and her daughter. There was no way I could approach this family without understanding and appreciating the political climate, the zeitgeist that provided the framework of our realities. The uncles' main complaint and one on which they all agreed in spite of their personal differences was "what do the youth of today think? Just because we overthrew a dictator and cheered for freedom that doesn't mean we will forgo our religious and cultural standards". The rebel teenage girl smiled shrewdly, and I had to conceal just how fascinated I was by her clear-sightedness. She knew where she was going and I felt that my role was to help the mother safely navigate her daughter through this. Her rebellious approach may backfire and the situation she was in was more favorable towards her uncles than it was towards mother and daughter.

The brothers could have their sister hospitalized for being in a manic episode of her bipolar depression. While she was in hospital, for months at a time, they would take control over the teenage daughter, keeping her in check, restricting her movements, inside the house and out. This was extremely frustrating to me. As a therapist, I felt weak and ineffectual, as a mother of a teenage daughter I could relate to the confusion of teenage hood and the pain of a mother not able to reach out. As a Libyan woman, I felt angry and bitter at men who could simply disenfranchise me in the absence of a functioning legal or social system. How could I possibly tease apart the politics from the circumstances this family was living in? I simply could not. When I shared this personal dilemma with our trainer, Laurie Charlés, she casually and matter-of-factly stated that, "all therapy is political"! That was one of a few Eureka moments I have had in my life. I am continuously reminded of the value of this statement, resonating in almost all therapeutic as well as other settings I find myself working in.

Working through issues with families often brings politics into the therapeutic context. The backdrop of people's experience always comes to the forefront once a problem is identified; it seems like a natural side effect of the therapeutic process. Recent and current events act like a code for understanding the antecedents and maintaining factors of, for instance, substance abuse or PTSD; when a father complains that his ex-combatant son smokes more than 20 joints a day to numb the pain or a mother conveys that her warrior son can only sleep holding onto his machine gun. Once families are able to describe these issues, the main theme of the session invariably becomes the present political situation.

Interestingly, families often use the safety of the session to discuss what at times are deep-seated political differences. It seems that factors like the agreed upon condition of mutual respect, the physical setting, sitting an equal distance apart and getting an equal opportunity to be heard and to listen to others, all provide the ideal conditions for constructive dialogue. I have often thought that it is precisely these terms and conditions that need to be applied to our political discourse. Libya seems to be in the control of people who have not learned to communicate in a constructive manner; similar to a family that begins to struggle when boundaries become fuzzy and roles and responsibilities are compromised.

Reality Check: Working Under the Powers that Be The realization that politics cannot be severed from our experience, as individuals grappling with personal challenges, nor can it be severed from our experience collectively, as a nation in need of help, brought with it the added responsibility that comes with knowledge. In August 2014, as I sat in my office at the clinic in Tripoli, talking with a woman who was complaining that she felt guilty about neglecting her family. She had no desire to socialize or interact with her husband and children because she was constantly worried and anxious about the ongoing civil war that had reignited a couple of weeks earlier. She felt she had failed as a mother as she could not protect her children and loved ones from impending harm.

As I tried to reassure her that she was safe at this moment, sitting here with me in the office, that together we could explore ways to help her manage her fears, and regain some sense of worth within her family, I could hear heavy shelling not too far in the distance. As I struggled to find a way to impart some sense of security, the first thing that came to mind was the concept of genuineness (Cormier and Hackney 2012). I must have come across like a complete hypocrite to my client; we could both hear the blasts outside. Who was I fooling by trying to establish a safe environment that would allow us to build a relationship of trust when danger was clearly only a few kilometers away? This thinking casts a shadow on all our helping efforts. It renders us helpless, untrustworthy and weak at the mercy of people who decide to stretch their mighty "arms" whenever and however they please. It did cross my mind that what I was trying to do was futile and I might as well pack up and leave.

I could easily rationalize my way out of this. Still I kept going; it was not a conscious decision to be strong in the face adversity or anything as glamorous as that. I was going from one appointment to the next; the thought of not going to the clinic in these times just did not sit well, and I kept telling myself that I would stop doing this when I am no longer any use to anyone. I realized later that I needed these interactions as a means of self-soothing treatment, by reassuring families that there are workable ways around these hurdles, the uncertainty, the fear, the loss of control, I was essentially reinforcing what I needed to do with my own family during difficult times.

The Versatility of Family Therapy

At the time I started thinking about this chapter, I was asked by a friend and ex-colleague at an international organization to join a psychosocial support team that was working with IDPs in Kurdistan, northern Iraq. Earlier in the chapter, I mentioned my growing realization of how the training had shaped my professional life and how I related to humanitarian work. That influence became even more evident when I started working again under very similar circumstances yet in a different country with its unique characteristics. This experience is enriching because it builds on a bond that I had previously been unaware of, namely the bond between family therapy and humanitarian work.

I am currently in Kurdistan, working with IDPs and family therapy interventions inevitably became the order of the day. I am visiting IDPs in their camps, individuals who are referred by the psychosocial team as needing help with how they are coping and the difficulties they face. In a tent or caravan with families consisting of, at times, up to 10 individuals, family therapy was almost unavoidable. With temperatures of 45 °C outside and with almost no shaded areas, only on very rare occasions could I ask the remaining family members to leave so I could have some privacy in discussing very sensitive and personal issues with a specific family member. I immediately became aware that, once again, the experience of IDPs could only be fully appreciated within the context of the family and the system this family was currently forced to exist in. I mentally reached into my FT toolbox and hoped that the same tools could be applied even if I did not fully understand the sociopolitical factors involved.

The politics of this region are so complex and I was daunted by trying to make sense of why this country was in so much turmoil. I felt that I would have to resort to my own experience of displacement in order to connect with the people I was trying to help. Since I could not grasp the politics that caused this displacement, I decided there was no point in going after the "Why?" I remembered that one of my favorite trainers drilled the idea that it was more valuable to explore the emotional aspect of people's experiences, the "How?" and "What?" of our thoughts and feelings (Van der Veer, personal communication 2013). I have found this approach to be invaluable as it instantly generates the empathy required for a healthy therapeutic relationship.

Furthermore, I have realized that a few very basic interventions work best in the most difficult times. "Your reaction is a normal response to abnormal circumstances". These words still sound like music to my ears. The message is simple, the content empowering, and the effect liberating. It conveys the following normalizing thought: "what you are feeling is OK, it's alright to feel this way, and you are not weak or abnormal. Many others in this situation feel the same way". By saying these things, I regain some of my above-mentioned damaged genuineness because I believe that they can change the way a person perceives him or herself. When I express that these reactions, no matter how strange they seem, are normal considering the circumstances, I see an immediate effect of recognition and relief.

By validating their reactions people feel understood and accepted. This is the only way we can start to build trust in a therapeutic relationship where personal strengths are rediscovered and hope is instilled, making the desired change more attainable.

The last two years have provided me with the opportunity to get acquainted with family therapy, to receive and then deliver this intervention in a humanitarian context necessitated by the political developments on the ground. As a beginner professional, I have found that family therapy interventions are widely applicable as they are pragmatic and versatile. I never expected that family therapy would play such an important role in the work I do. My initial apprehension has been replaced by the acceptance that it is an important component in linking the helping profession with humanitarian work. Furthermore, this development has also helped me assimilate the fact that politics of war not only affect our physical reality, but rather by weakening our sense of efficacy also pervade our psychological wellbeing. Once people become vulnerable, regardless of who or where they are, those of us who have the ability to help with specialized services, and are offered a possibility to reach out, will find it hard to look away. Whether this involvement is defined as humanitarian work, psychological interventions or psychosocial support is inconsequential.

References

Bateson, G. (1972). *Steps to an ecology of mind*. San Francisco, CA: Chandler.
Charles, L. (2013). *Personal Communication*. Tripoli, Libya.
Cormier, S., & Hackney, H. (2012). *Counseling strategies and interventions* (8th ed.). Upper Saddle River, NJ: Pearson.
Franklin, C., Trepper, T. S., McCollum, E. E., & Gingerich, W. J. (Eds.). (2012). *Solution-focused brief therapy: A handbook of evidence-based practice*. New York, NY: Oxford University Press.
Haley, J., & Richeport-Haley, M. (2007). *Directive family therapy*. New York, NY: Hawthorne.
van der Veer (2013). *Personal Communication*. Tripoli, Libya.
von Bertalanffy, L. (1968). *General system theory: Foundations, development, applications*. New York, NY: George Brazilla.

"My Son Is Alive": Is Family Therapy Appropriate for Families of the Disappeared in Sri Lanka?

Gameela Samarasinghe

Introduction

Hundreds of people in Sri Lanka have had similar experiences as those described to me by Mrs. X.[1] Her son disappeared while in combat. With her consent, I am sharing parts of her life story, thoughts about family, family therapy, reconciliation and coping while engaging in a discussion on how in Sri Lanka, families deal with ambiguous loss and whether family therapy can in any way support families of the disappeared during reconciliation processes. It is through Mrs. X's experiences that I discuss these issues.

I am a Clinical Psychologist by training who felt that it was necessary to shelve all that I had learned at the Sorbonne when I began work in Sri Lanka 25 years ago. I needed to start from scratch in order to get a better understanding of how people in Sri Lanka described their experiences and suffering. My training and books did not give me answers. My work has mainly focused on studying the psychosocial impacts of conflicts on individuals and communities. It led me to interact with and talk to many people who have been directly and indirectly affected by the war from 1983 to 2009 and by the political violence that took place in the late 1980s.[2] Mrs. X. was one person I met while engaged in research. When I was recently appointed by the Government to serve on a task force to set up and implement public consultations on reconciliation mechanisms, I immediately thought of contacting Mrs. X. with the hope that she would agree to share her ideas about expectations from commissions and describe the hopes and fears they trigger especially in families of the disappeared.

---

[1]Mrs. X. to ensure confidentiality. I thank her for sharing her story and permitting me to quote her.
[2]The Janatha Vimukthi Peramuna (JVP) insurrection between 1987 and 1989.

G. Samarasinghe (✉)
University of Colombo, Colombo, Sri Lanka
e-mail: gameela2010@gmail.com

Even though I have known Mrs. X. for many years, I had not had an opportunity to ask her about her experiences of loss, suffering and coping as well as her thoughts on reconciliation. We had talked several times at meetings and conferences to do with the families of the disappeared or regarding women's empowerment, issues that are very close to Mrs. X's heart. When I called her to make an appointment to meet with her, she very willingly agreed to talk to me. We spent a couple of hours together while she relived her painful experience, a story she has told many over and over again.

Commissions for the Families of the Disappeared

Tens of thousands of people in Sri Lanka have been forcibly disappeared. Amongst them are Sinhalese youth who were suspected of links to the Janatha Vimukthi Peramuna (JVP). They were targets in the late 1980s and early 1990s. Throughout the long armed conflict between government forces and the Liberation Tigers of Tamil Eelam (LTTE) that finally ended in May 2009, personnel from the armed forces like Mrs. X's son as well as Tamil civilians and LTTE cadre disappeared. Muslims (both activists and prominent community members) have been suspected victims of enforced disappearances too. Others including journalists and activists are also missing to date.

Since 1990, governments have launched nine presidential commissions to address the problem of enforced disappearances. None have brought families of the disappeared any closer to truth or justice. In 2013, the former government established a Presidential Commission[3] to Investigate into Complaints regarding missing persons (COI). Families of the disappeared went before the Commission in thousands with the hope of finding their family members who had disappeared. Dreading the outcome of the hearing, families would appear before a commission. They wanted to know if their family member was alive or dead, or if still alive, they feared he may have been tortured in a secret detention camp. It was the truth that they sought.

They say that the Commission has not made any progress towards truth seeking even after they went themselves and requested the government to reform the Commission. Because of their disillusionment and the continuation of their pain and suffering, they voted for the change of government, with the hope that their voices will be heard but even today they still feel very frustrated that their situation has remained the same. As a sign of protest they boycotted the public hearings of the Commission in Jaffna that were held from 11th to 17th December 2015 and asked the government to create a meaningful and effective mechanism that will enable them to seek truth and justice.[4]

---

[3]Maxwell Parakrama Paranagama Commission.

[4]Families of the disappeared, 8th December 2015—http://groundviews.org/2015/12/11/appeal-by-the-families-of-the-disappeared/.

When the COI was established, the hope of the people was evident. From all parts of Sri Lanka, an impressive number of families sent complaints and others travelled to be heard. Initially the mandate of the Commission was to investigate into complaints regarding missing persons from 1990 to 2009 in the North and East. The COI emphasized the importance of truth telling and its implications towards justice, accountability and reconciliation in Sri Lanka. But later the mandate of the COI expanded covering the period 1983–2009, from the beginning of the war to its end, and included violations of international humanitarian law and international human rights law. "Critiques of the broadening of the mandate pointed out that the issue of disappearances became secondary" (Fonseka 2015). The timing of the establishment of the Commission, just before the international investigation established in accordance with the UNHRC resolution was also perceived more as a political move to satisfy the international community rather than giving greater importance to addressing disappearances (Fonseka 2015).[5]

"For many families of the disappeared the COI was yet another Commission Mrs. X. says, yet another opportunity to hope for the truth". "People were allowed a few minutes to give brief statements before the Commission, a Commission whose members did not know how to respond and support them while they relived the pain of losing their family members. They simply ended up losing faith that the Commission could give them any answers to their questions". Mrs. X. spoke about these families with empathy, as someone who understood what they went through, having appeared before other commissions previously when trying to understand the fate of her son.

Truth for Reconciliation

Mrs. X. confirms that truth is what people want. "Everyone wants the truth" she says, "not only the families of the missing people. Once the truth is established, then justice will be sought for reconciliation". In her case, her son was in the Sri Lankan army. She is still living in hope that her son will return. He disappeared 17 years ago. She keeps chocolates in the fridge and soap in the bathroom in case he comes back. She says: "a murder is different, you grieve, you mourn, it is over. Until I die, it is still there." In the case of disappearances in the North and East of civilians, she says, "someone might have seen that they were picked up, and then you can guess what might have happened".

In her own way, Mrs. X. is working towards reconciliation, reconciliation within herself and reconciliation with those who might have taken her son's life. Courageously and tirelessly, for almost two decades, she has been supporting other women who have experienced similar situations. She works with women from the

---

[5]http://groundviews.org/2014/08/12/prioritising-truth-in-post-war-sri-lanka/.

North and East as well. One of them told her that 'she had to run with her 11 month old child leaving her 3 year old child to die, that she had to run because of the soldiers'. This was an eye opener for Mrs. X, the turning point she said. She says: "my son was carrying a gun." He might have been one of those soldiers. Today, she expresses no anger towards the perpetrators, who ever they are. She works with all families who have lost a member. And like all these families, she is still waiting.

In the Sri Lankan context it is sometimes difficult to use the term 'Reconciliation' since the term Reconciliation may not comprise of all options necessary to meet the needs of people who had experienced psychological suffering or human rights violations. It may also not be a term that is understood by people in general. Reconciliation as a word also carries nuances of compulsory forgiveness, forgetting and/or resignation, which may not be the appropriate framework within which to work when dealing with psychosocially distressed individuals and communities. Additionally, different processes may be involved in 'reconciling' within oneself, 'reconciling' amongst individuals and communities and 'reconciling' between communities.

Appropriate and effective redress will significantly contribute towards helping people move on within their lives as well as towards helping communities to come to terms with and traverse their collective experiences[6] (Salih and Samarasinghe 2006).

Currently, reconciliation is mostly discussed in relation to accountability, compensation for victims and their families, truth and justice. Truth, as expressed by Mrs. X. and in the statement by the Families of the Disappeared is a critical part in the journey towards reconciliation.

By reconciliation, it is implied that communities need to engage and eventually live peacefully together. Not everyone is forgiving like Mrs. X. It is necessary to ask what reconciliation means to individuals who have suffered the consequences of the war in terms of their impacts on themselves, their families and their community. Do the processes eventually lead to forgiveness of the perpetrators? Is forgiveness the ultimate aim of the reconciliation process? How will affected persons be consulted prior to establishing mechanisms involved? Some affected persons have expressed the need for confidentiality and psychosocial support during submissions before commissions/transitional justice processes and also to consult with perpetrators as they could help construct the truth. Language[7] is also an issue. Those who have been affected need to speak to people who can understand what they say and are familiar with their area and issues. Yet, usually the social, economic and educational distance between people appointed to Commissions are such that people are intimidated and this can affect their submissions.

---

[6]Excerpts from Localizing Transitional Justice in the Context of Psychosocial Work in Sri Lanka, Salih and Samarasinghe, published by Social Policy Analysis and Research Centre (SPARC), University of Colombo, October 2006.

[7]In Sri Lanka, the local languages are Sinhala and Tamil. The more educated people, like the potential members of the Commission would feel more comfortable speaking in English.

Mrs. X. stated that families she works with felt that the people serving on Commissions have not demonstrated genuine empathy and concern for what they have experienced. She says, women in particular have felt uncomfortable speaking openly to commission members mostly consisting of men. They are also very aware that the members should not consist of anyone from the army, police or government officials. Local persons (academics or other) were their preference, people who would understand how they lived. It was also important to them that the hearings would take place where they would feel comfortable, in the Divisional Secretariat level for example.

Mrs. X. stated that emotional and social support before, during and following the consultations is a necessity. "People who have lost their loved ones need to cry and tell personal stories", she said. Mrs. X. went on to say that "commissions have to be prepared to deal with and respond to their emotions. Ideally someone with a psychosocial training should either serve on the committee or provide guidance and expertise to the members of the committee. There should also be a person who is accessible and speaks their language, who can be contacted by the victims at any point in time, should they want to add or delete information in their statements. Of course, their security must be guaranteed and in no way should they be intimidated after they have given their submission." "Most people", Mrs. X. says, "have been waiting for years for some response after they have appeared before commissions. They want action, and fast. For example, for missing family members, they do not want death certificates anymore. They want a certificate of absence.[8]"

As stated in the discussion paper on the certificate of absence by the Centre for Policy Alternatives (CPA), a certificate of absence can affirm the status of 'missing' as opposed to 'deceased'. It will address certain practical issues such as property transfer, access to compensation etc. But it can also help family members of the disappeared emotionally and psychologically without dismissing the need for active investigation into cases of the disappeared and holding the government accountable to continue with the investigation.

Commissions and the Complexities of Ambiguous Loss

Family therapists reading this volume, and this chapter, will recognize the nature of loss that is currently being dealt with in Sri Lanka. Families of the disappeared who appear before Commissions are dealing with what is termed ambiguous loss, "the most stressful loss because its incomprehensibility threatens health and resiliency." The people they care about have disappeared physically or are fading away psychologically (Boss 2006, p. 22).

"It seems that across situations and cultures, the ambiguity of missing persons blocks grief, seeds ambivalence, guilt, relational conflict, and blurs family

---

[8]http://www.cpalanka.org/wp-content/uploads/2015/09/Certificates-of-Absence-FINAL.pdf.

boundaries and processes. Families are often so preoccupied with the lost person that those present—especially children and adolescents—are ignored." (Boss 2006, p. 21). In addition, a disappearance often involves multiple losses not only of life, but also of property, livelihood and even dreams for the future (Walsh 2007). For example, Mrs. X's two other sons have done well but she is still constantly reminded of the son she lost, focusing mostly on him when she talks. "When I hear a bulldozer I get affected physically", "I had watched a documentary that the Liberation Tigers of Tamil Eelam (LTTE) had released to see if I could recognize my son's face amongst the dead bodies".

Events of this nature impact on interactions between family members. They affect thought, feelings and their sense of agency, as well as reduced social involvement, diminished interest in life, feelings of social detachment (Saul 2014), "I cry alone not to alarm my family because I don't want my family to know that I am still in pain". Mrs. X. says her lifestyle changed completely. She used to entertain colleagues and friends quite a lot before her son disappeared. Disappearances often involve loss of resources as well (Saul 2014). Her husband was a businessman but "all that has gone". She cannot read anymore. Before, she couldn't fall asleep without reading a book, even a cookery book, she said. Now she doesn't sleep well, never slept alone after the loss, doesn't even read the newspapers. She says her self control is less, she gets more angry. She has severed contact with her family members who did not get in touch with her after her son disappeared. "When they were most needed, they were not there".

Families with missing members are searching for meaning. They need to make sense of what happened to the person who disappeared, to themselves and perhaps to the country, to find a rational reasoning about what happened. It took Mrs. X. years to arrive at her present psychological state. Although her sleep is still affected, she is able to work effectively. She says that "her search for an explanation of what happened to her son and under what circumstances he disappeared, was only possible because of the support she got from her family and friends." She describes it as "a long and never ending painful process" but "the reality hit her one day, all of a sudden". For Mrs. X, the realization that her son was carrying a gun and that he was a perpetrator as was the person who killed him, helped her look at life differently. After 'coming to terms' with her loss, she is devoting her life to work with families of the disappeared. She lives to support them. She prepares them to face forthcoming commissions as she is aware of what she had to endure on earlier occasions. She asks herself: "Are commissions equipped to listen to the distress of families and help them find a positive meaning in their trauma and loss? Are families ready to hear whether their loved one is alive or dead? How do families function when they are not given an acceptable response, a solution by the commission? And if the commission has records that indicate that a person is in fact dead, how is this told to his family members? How are families supported as they deal with information that in a moment nullifies all their hopes of finding the missing family member? Can family therapy be helpful to families of the disappeared in Sri Lanka? Is there relevance for family therapy in the postwar context of Sri Lanka?

Family Therapy for Families of the Disappeared in Sri Lanka

The Sri Lankan family unit is fluid with the extended family and the community village each playing different roles. There are many different contexts in which the individual lives: as a partner in a couple relationship, as a family member, a person with cultural and/or religious beliefs, while also taking into consideration socio-economic circumstances and political processes.

For example, Mrs. X. explained to me how her relationships with her family members had got disrupted after the loss of her son. Relatives who had been close to her, behaved in ways she could not comprehend. Some, whom she considered close to her did not contact her or sympathise with her after the news was out about the disappearance of her son. She felt she was being alienated by her family and the community. Her grief was hers and could not be shared with others. She said that "people in her village thought she was 'mad'. She was able to survive that period of her life because of her close family who supported her".

Mrs. X.'s experience soon after her loss demonstrates that the family can indeed be a great source of support but also of distress when some family members misunderstand the pain and suffering following a disappearance. Boss confirms that families often perceive the situation differently and this can lead to rifts and alienations (Boss and Yeats 2014).

Generally speaking any situation or a problem that affects relationships among family members and family functioning and its supportive role, can benefit from systemic family therapy (Boss and Yeats 2014). Any problem of an individual that affects his life in relation to his relationships to family and wider contexts will benefit too (Saul 2014). Family therapy can certainly improve family functioning at different levels; enhancement of mutual understanding and emotional support among family members, development of coping skills and problem solving strategies in various dilemmas and situations. Family therapy rests on systemic assumptions or a contextual perspective which emphasizes the role of wider systems such as the community, the society and the culture to which the family belongs. Attention must be given to the impact of wider systems and social contexts on people's lives, especially in contexts such as disappearances in Sri Lanka.

Interventions are currently taking place in Sri Lanka for families of the disappeared, usually with more than one family member. As Boss and Yeats state, enabling family members to use their resources in a supportive way was found to be vital in helping members manage transitional stages of family development or stressful life events such as serious illness or a death of a family member. They can work on how to reshape family traditions that might have got lost after the disappearance or how to normalize the ambivalence felt due to the ambiguous loss, improve communication between family members, and help find a meaning to what happened to the family (Boss and Yeats 2014).

Yet, Somasundaram (2014) states that "more fundamental problems at the family and collective levels need to be addressed before individuals recover. First societal and community trust, relationships, structures and institutions have to be rebuilt. Threat, fear and terror are experienced at the family and community levels. As a result the way the family functions changes. When trying to help, it is important to understand the wider ramifications and intervene to rectify the adverse changes at the family and collective levels and then individuals recover within the nurturing environment" (p. li). Mrs. X. appreciates some initiatives on the part of the government to address the needs of the families of the disappeared at a collective level. She says there is a "need for tracing the missing person, legal support and mental health care. When a relative dies, a death certificate is issued and with it, families are able to move forward. They can apply for compensation, attend to property transfer or get re-married if this is their wish." She suggested that if the government issues a certificate of absence,[9] that would affirm the status of 'disappeared' as opposed to 'deceased'. "The certificate of absence would balance family members' emotional and psychological needs without dismissing the need for active investigation into cases of disappearances" (CPA 2015). "Restoring social trust becomes one of the greatest challenges for survivors of collective trauma[10] and often takes the form of demands for acknowledgement, accountability, and justice" (Saul 2014).

This may go beyond the scope of family therapy. In providing a space for families of the disappeared to seek the truth, Commissions are 'unknowingly' attempting to restore an environment that will impact positively on the wellbeing of the community, family and the individual. These Commissions need to be prepared to support families through this process.

Practitioners can also assist by promoting wellbeing and resilience. When there is a disappearance, an inevitable consequence is the "shared injuries to a population's social, cultural, and physical ecologies" (Saul 2014). It is a "blow to the basic tissues of social life that damages the bonds attaching people together and impairs the prevailing sense of communality.... It is a form of shock all the same, a gradual realization that the community no longer exists as an effective source of support" (Erikson 1976). Indeed, in the case of Sri Lanka's families of the disappeared, the community has remained shattered making it all the more difficult for the individual to recover and motivating him to desperately seek truth when any opportunity to be heard arises. There is a need to strengthen the adaptive capacities or resilience in families and communities, as they promote collective recovery after mass trauma. "Collective recovery is a creative and emergent process; its content and form are constructed over time through cycles of collective action, reflection and narration" (Saul 2014).

In Sri Lanka, individuals who have suffered the consequences of the war do not perceive therapy as particularly helpful or a matter of urgency when their priorities are to feed their families or educate their children. Going for therapy means travelling long distances for sessions. People have to often deprive themselves of their

---

[9]http://www.cpalanka.org/wp-content/uploads/2015/09/Certificates-of-Absence-FINAL.pdf.
[10]Collective trauma describes the impact of massive trauma on the family and community.

daily wage and ensure that their children are cared for while they go for therapy. Working with families in Sri Lanka, and particularly with families of the disappeared, is even more of a challenge. There are no family therapists yet, only a few psychiatrists and psychologists. Because of the dearth of mental health professionals and the extent of the problem in terms of numbers[11] and where the families live, attention must be given to the impacts of wider systems and social contexts.

Currently, strategies to support families of the disappeared, such as social support programs are being designed and carried out. The social approach has been found to be more effective than any attempts at Family Therapy in Sri Lanka. Groups of mothers and wives of the disappeared as well as groups of fathers and brothers have been formed in every district in the country where families of the disappeared were located. They meet and talk about the issues they have faced and how they cope. Different family members give different meanings to the loss. There are open disputes when one family member believes that the disappeared member is dead and others think he is still alive.

While these issues and interventions are likely to be familiar to readers, it is interesting that in Sri Lanka, the setting in which these issues are discussed is not in the context of a family therapy session. Of particular note is the role of the psychosocial support community in ensuring that distressed individuals and communities are supported in articulating their needs regarding the form and framework of the desired process for redressing grievances and human rights violations and reconciliation, in ensuring that these processes are implemented and later in helping people access and go through the required procedures.

Family tensions also arise when the focus is only on the missing, who invariably is the best person in the family. Meaning about the loss is often found through religion. People who believe that the disappeared person is still alive will do alms giving, Hindus will pray. Others will perform rituals or activities to keep the missing person alive such as planting trees or posting posters on bus stands. This 'social intervention' is perceived as reaching out to communities rather than individuals and appears to be more meaningful to families whose family members have disappeared. This form of collective action opens opportunities for reflection and narration. It addresses traumas at family and collective levels before responding to them at the level of the individual.

Conclusion

Families of the disappeared need to appear before commissions that are 'therapeutic' not commissions that will further increase their distress. Many people, have been disappointed that they did not get answers to their questions. Where is their

---

[11]16,000 disappearances have been registered with the ICRC in Sri Lanka (ICRC, personal communication, December 10, 2015).

loved one? Is he dead or is he alive? Due to the uncertainty about whether their family member is alive or dead, families have suffered from ambiguous loss. Commissions have been unprepared to respond to the questions and to deal with families' distress, leaving them in a state of limbo.

Persons distressed by their experiences will require support to share their experiences and opinions. For example, people living in the various conflict-affected areas of Sri Lanka may find it unsafe to name perpetrators, to describe their experiences and to share their hopes for justice and reconciliation. Extreme caution has to be taken to ensure the safety and security of respondents when undertaking any attempt to access people's hopes and aspirations for feelings of justice and for reconciliation following their experience of violation" (Charlés and Samarasinghe 2015).

The psychosocial sector in Sri Lanka has no expertise in Family Therapy. However, it recognizes the importance the role family relationships can play in the recovery process of families of the disappeared. This paper argues however, that in the case of Sri Lanka, and in particular in relation to the families of the disappeared, that it is important to consider a broader framework for support, that first attempts to respond to collective, societal concerns and gradually moves to family relationships and eventually reaches the individual. Family therapists interested in working and understanding reconciliation mechanisms in post war countries also must recognize the nature in which these instruments exist.

References

Boss, P. (2006). *Loss, trauma, and resilience: Therapeutic work with ambiguous loss*. New York, NY: Norton.
Boss, P., & Yeats, J. R. (2014). Ambiguous loss: A complicated type of grief when loved ones disappear. *Bereavement Care, 33*(2), 63–69.
Centre for Policy Alternatives. (2015). *Certificates of absence: A practical step to address challenges faced by the families of the disappeared in Sri Lanka [discussion paper]*. Colombo, Sri Lanka: Centre for Policy Alternatives.
Charlés, L., & Samarasinghe, G. (2015). Psychosocial innovations in post-war Sri Lanka. Retrieved from http://www.taosinstitute.net/psychosocial-innovation-in-post-war-sri-lanka/.
Erikson, K. (1976). *Everything in its path: Destruction of community in the Buffalo Creek flood*. New York, NY: Simon & Schuster.
Fonseka, B. (2015). Prioritising truth in post-war Sri Lanka. Retrieved from http://www.groundviews.org/2014/08/12/prioritising-truth-in-post-war-sri-lanka/.
Salih, M., & Samarasinghe, G. (2006). *Localizing transitional justice in the context of psychosocial work in Sri Lanka*. Colombo, Sri Lanka: Social Policy Analysis and Research Centre, University of Colombo.
Saul, J. (2014). *Collective trauma collective healing: Promoting community resilience in the aftermath of disaster*. New York, NY: Routledge.
Somasundaram, D. (2014). *Scarred communities: Psychosocial impact of man-made and natural disasters on Sri Lankan society*. New Delhi, India: Sage.
Walsh, F. (2007). Traumatic loss and major disasters: Strengthening family and community resilience. *Family Process, 46*(2), 207–227.

Kaleidoscopic Shifts: The Development of New Understandings as Therapists "Go and Find out"

Catalina Perdomo, Deborah Healy, Daisy Ceja, Kathryn Dunne and Kotia Whitaker

Where It All Started

The story we tell here began in September, 2014, when one of our peers had just begun her family therapy training at Our Lady of the Lake University (OLLU), in the Master's program in Family, Couple, and Individual Psychotherapy. Yajaira's first class was Life Span Development. Here are our colleague's reflections:

> I wondered what my professor would be like. I then met Dr. Laurie Lopez Charlés. I was woo'ed with her personality and world experience, intrigued by her life and wanted to know more. I began staying after class more and more days to ask her questions about how she got involved with the work she talked about in class. I have always had a passion for learning about different cultures and places. My father instilled that in me at a very early age with his stories of Nahuals and Tapirs in Panama. Dr. Laurie continues to feed that passion with her mentorship of me. From all these questions, and the passion of Dr. Laurie, our "Shoufi Mafi," a family therapy student working group in global mental health, was born (Charlés 2015). Shoufi Mafi means "what's up" in Arabic. We are a group of university students at OLLU, who share a passion for learning ways to work domestically and internationally in the context of family therapy. In this chapter, some of us from this student work group share our reflections, impressions, and emergent understandings that continue to inform our clinical growth as future marriage and family therapists, looking both inside and beyond our training in the U.S.

C. Perdomo (✉) · D. Healy · D. Ceja · K. Dunne · K. Whitaker
Our Lady of the Lake University, San Antonio, TX, USA
e-mail: cperdomo@ollusa.edu

© American Family Therapy Academy 2016
L.L. Charlés and G. Samarasinghe (eds.), *Family Therapy in Global Humanitarian Contexts*, AFTA SpringerBriefs in Family Therapy,
DOI 10.1007/978-3-319-39271-4_11

The First Leap of Faith: The Mongoose Imperative

Deborah Healy, PsyD

Could Kipling (1894) have imagined postmodern therapists when he constructed the "mongoose-imperative" that repeatedly sent Rikki Tikki Tavi on a mission to "to go and find out"? He wrote: "It is the hardest thing in the world to frighten a mongoose, because he is eaten up from nose to tail with curiosity." Perhaps, clinical curiosity requires boldness and bravery too: the courage to occupy the "not knowing stance", the willingness to surrender our own knowing in deference to the client's, the leap of faith that sends practitioners to far-off lands, and the assertiveness to roll up our sleeves, and to commit to engaging in respectful and collaborative therapeutic interactions.

In order to provide a contextual backdrop, I offer the following: I am a faculty member and The Training Director of the Counseling Psychology Doctoral Program at Our Lady of the Lake University. As a counseling psychologist trained in systemic and marriage and family traditions, living and working in the United States, I am aware that my clinical perspective and counseling experiences are keenly and insidiously shaped by demographic variables: age, training, culture, geographic location, and more. These descriptors inform both my active and passive vision—in other words, how I see and how I am seen. These are some of my lenses through which I view the world. Yet, simultaneously, I am reminded of the *mighty kaleidoscope*, in which the smallest shift of the lens, the most delicate turn of the visual field, changes everything!

The experience of the student working group, our Shoufi-Mafi in global mental health, provided kaleidoscopic moments for me and for the masters-level family therapy students at Our Lady of the Lake University. The group turned the visual field with a gentle hand by inviting us into dialogue about the provision of mental health services across global contexts. Hence, I have been the virtual traveler. I did not go physically, yet I have traversed psychologically, professionally, and emotionally–propelled by our interactions, conversations, questions and emergent, fluid, and socially-negotiated, understandings.

As each conversation initiated more shifts, the student working group of Shoufi Mafi and I decided to engage in free and unstructured writing to both liberate and capture our curiosities and to explore our own notions and biases about working in humanitarian contexts. The writing process was sometimes raw, reverberating the energy of other migration stories, the role and rights of women, the preservation of the role of the therapist against the possibility of being viewed as an interloper or unwelcome interventionist.

I was somewhat surprised by these themes and have listened with great admiration as my co-authors have strategically journeyed through the muck and mire of many ideological struggles including: Guilt–(regarding providing services in other lands—fueled by the fear of interventionism and the inherent power differentials between the American-trainee and the families in nations visited by relief organizations), Gender-Biases, and the myriad potential effects of being helped.

The students and I have used this experience to metabolize our own uncertainties and trepidations and to gather our collective courage to one day implement humanitarian mental health provision with grace, respect, and reflection; acknowledging that helping changes us, too.

Prior to coming to teach at the university, much of my early work was in direct services to children and teenagers in the USA. Later my work involved program leadership, intentionally structuring initiatives and directing staff who were engaged in counseling, mental health first aid, crisis response, prevention of high risk behaviors and systems-work aimed at the development of youth resiliency. My programmatic scope encompassed direct responsibility for staff who, on a daily basis, served more than 100,000 children and teens in one of the largest public school districts in this southern region of Texas. It is commonly accepted here that children and teens are a valuable and yet *vulnerable* population who deserve early and consistent support and guidance in order to avert mental health concerns in later life.

Now, after dialogues with my colleagues, I have begun to wonder if this sense of "safeguarding" the future through youth prevention would be as prevalent in the USA if our daily survival was threatened by war and terrorism fought in our local streets and neighborhoods, and by the chronic scarcity of basic survival resources. I am now newly curious about the temporal aspects of clinical urgency–how can prevention be urgent when families are grappling with the immediacy of survival? How do these temporal aspects (survival now versus transgenerational health later), inform our therapeutic emphases? Must practitioners be pushed to the forced-choice "either/or" position in lands where resources are scarce and survival is chronically threatened? Is prevention-work a luxury, perhaps, a by-product of safety and stability? What implications might this have for trainees and practitioners alike?

My curiosity has spawned this first theme of therapeutic focus which I will call: the "now or the later". Must it be "either/or"; could there be a "both/and" (Andersen 1997) focus? It would seem that the environment sets the priorities by its level of challenge to survival. I witnessed some of this urgency in the aftermath of Hurricane Katrina and the attacks upon New York City after September 11, 2001.

Another recurrent and recursive theme for me during these months, has been related to the very nature of clinical curiosity itself. As a child in the USA, I remember being told that "curiosity killed the cat". Nevertheless, I cannot stop wondering what curiosity can do for the therapeutic process. Unlike cats, the clinical curiosities of mental health practitioners are tempered within boundaries of training, theory, ethics, and respect for the full-spectrum of understandings that our clients co-construct with us and with others in their social worlds.

Therefore, my next curiosity turns the kaleidoscope once again, as I challenge much of what I think I know. One Thursday afternoon, as the students and I gathered around a computer screen, we listened intently to a psychologist ("Eva") half way around the world (via Skype) describing her work in the midst of armed conflict in her country. At that moment, my curiosity was "jump started" by her disclosures and her accompanying vibrancy. I wanted to "go and find out". Eva's face radiated joy when she explained that she has a water delivery every ten days and electricity for two hours a day. Although such circumstances are common in settings like Eva's, for me, this was a surprise. I wondered if I could be as strong and as focused as she. Her overarching gratitude was palpable. She was grateful for the resources that support her work. I felt decidedly root-bound in my understandings of my work as a psychologist. I have taken resources for granted, as an entitlement, as the default. I had not been personally curious (until that moment) about therapeutic work in low-resource settings. My curiosity had been academic; Eva's face made it personal. Perhaps, my leap of faith is to accept this naiveté and understand that rootedness doesn't have to mean being place-bound geographically. I can be rooted in my commitment and passion for psychotherapy, and expand the reach of these services to global contexts. This theme can be "both/and."

During these months I have wondered, does curiosity require a hierarchical "permission-ing?" Is it regulated by tradition, expectations, sensors that perceive threats, protective factors that keep the curious cats away? This has spawned a sideline conversation about this (a tributary dialogue) about clinical curiosity itself—(meta-curiosity) about the nature, texture, scope, content and veritable architecture of curiosity conjured on behalf of clients, practitioners and the process. For several months now, students and I have been eager to go and find out. Our conversations have been our means to traverse. We are finding out, step by step.

The Second Leap of Faith: Playing With Guilt

Catalina Perdomo

In order to share my story with you, I need you to know me. I am an emerging Family Therapist in my second year of the Family, Couple, and Individual Psychotherapy Master's Program at a private, Catholic university. I am also training under the Psychological Services for Spanish Speaking Populations certificate. My mother and father are first generation immigrants to the United States from Colombia, and I am the youngest of three. I consider myself a Spanish-English bilingual, a cis female Latina, and a proud dog mom. I joined Shoufi Mafi, our student working group in family therapy and global mental health, because I was interested in working internationally as a future psychologist, but I felt like I couldn't. Well, more so, I thought that I *shouldn't*. At first, I thought "how dare I, an American trained practitioner, carry my knowledge and force it on others?" Would coercion be involved? How could I guard against it? From my perspective, this helping effort could be received as so invasive, and, therefore, so guilt-inducing. Why guilt, I wondered? When I try to define this guilt, my Catholic upbringing is the first thing that comes to mind. I think of confessionals, priests, penances, and absolution. I think of my family.

My guilt reminds me of my family's history and the history of other families in similar contexts. I believed that because I was U.S. trained I didn't have a right to work with countries that may be facing problems that the U.S. had caused because of its involvement. When I reflect on Colombia's history with the U.S., I feel shame knowing that the relationship of exploitation extends all the way back to the Panama Canal in 1903. I felt stagnant in my guilt. How was exploitation able to force its way into Colombia and claim its treasures, continuing the tradition of conquistadors and colonists? I'm concerned that these colonists come in different forms and that they don't limit their reaping to canals or gold. They can force knowledge into non-consenting minds. I began to worry that by working internationally I might be vulnerable to continuing these patterns of force; that I might be guilty of becoming a colonist. This feeling of guilt developed into what I can only describe as perhaps being similar to my idea of white guilt when encountering white privilege. McIntosh (1988) in her essay, *White Privilege and Male Privilege*, provides us with a definition: "white privilege is like an invisible package of unearned assets that one can count on cashing in each day but about which one was 'meant' to remain oblivious." They are privileges earned solely on the basis of one's skin color. The white guilt that may come with white privilege can result in stagnation. Rothenberg (2002, p. 1) explains the experience as, "wallowing in guilt or moral outrage with no idea of how to move beyond them." To me, it's a floundering that occurs when I recognize a power or privilege differential and don't know what to do with it. A sensation somewhat similar to what Platt and Laszloffy (2013, p. 2) described: "Given that the majority of MFTs in the world are from the United States, asking them to consider the influence of nationality on clinical practice is like asking white people to consider how race informs their therapy with other white people."

As I struggled with this privilege, I also wrestled with naming it. I began switching back and forth between colonial and western guilt and still not finding a term for what I felt. Colonial guilt didn't fit because I understand it as a sensation of guilt for ravaging a country economically and capitalizing on their wealth through labor exploitation. Western guilt didn't sit quite well either because I only associated it with the U.S.' position of military and economic power over other countries. Perhaps I had to name it **Catalina's guilt**, and once I had named it I could move out of paralysis and toward action.

I then turned to my family for further understanding. This was all the more perplexing, because they are Colombian immigrants who have a personal history with the colonial exploitation I previously mentioned. In realizing my own intersections of countries, I began to consider my nationality as another dimension of diversity, and as a clinician in training, I began to consider the power differential between my nationality and my future clients' (Platt and Laszloffy 2013).

When I began my self-examination in my first year of my master's I was aware of the intersectionality of my identities, but I hadn't considered the intersections of my nationality as a part of that self-reflection. That began with the idea of Critical Patriotism (Platt and Laszloffy 2013). This was a process that was key in my training as a Spanish-bilingual therapist. Throughout my training translating is a daily task. Most of the time we work on translating English texts to Spanish, a chore that changes original U.S. or Western European authors' psychology articles or theories into new Spanish material. Things are lost and found in translations, but beginning with Western European or U.S. English articles or theories establishes the power differentials that place the English writers from the U.S. at the top of the hierarchy.

I believe my work as a Spanish-bilingual therapist-in-training perhaps lead me to become critically patriotic. I attribute this critical stance to constant google searches and confusion over DSM translations, hours of brainstorming how to ask systemic questions, and a supervisor who challenged us to eternally examine our language. I remember sitting in my Spanish Pre-Practicum class with our smartphones out googling translations: the frustration of never quite finding the right term or definition. We relied on each other to brainstorm how to ask the miracle question in Spanish, debated the use of "usted" and "tu", and ultimately roleplayed all of these interactions with the help of a native Spanish speaking supervisor.

In my personal development, my next step was to tackle the idea of cultural humility versus cultural competence (Tervalon and Murray-García 1998). In an effort to be culturally competent clinicians, we may be engaging in reinforcing stereotypes. By learning that Latin@s may face a disorder that is called "mal de ojo" in no way should that define "mal de ojo" as the same or even existing for all Latin@s. ("Mal de ojo" or "evil eye," is a supernatural illness that is sometimes defined as a stare that weakens the individual, invites bad luck, causes illness, and sometimes death. One common remedy is to pass a raw egg over the afflicted to absorb the curse) This is a catch of cultural competence that is easy to fall into. Instead, Tervalon and Murray-García (1998, p. 119) invite us, as trainees, to be "flexible and humble enough to let go of the false sense of security that stereotyping brings" and instead engage in a new experience with each client. This humility also encourages trainees who are expected to have knowledge to also admit when they don't. Perhaps this is another step towards the absolution of my guilt.

Throughout my master's studies I have read over and over again the importance of recognizing our positions of power whether it was from sexual orientation, gender, socio-economic status, or race. I would then try to take these concepts home to my Colombian parents and realize how contextually 'U.S.' these intersections can be.

So where did all of this leave me? It left me with the opportunity to transform 'Catalina's Guilt' into something positive. What is my guilt propelling me toward? Is the ultimate product of absolution respectful collaboration? Instead of allowing my guilt to produce disengagement I had to analyze this feeling on a continuum. As I reflect back on my explorations, I noticed that my first step was to name my struggle, to adopt a narrative practice of externalizing and naming my floundering as 'Catalina's Guilt'. By naming it I began to have conversations with colleagues; I took a position of change, and I learned to be honest with myself and others about my guilt. My next step, which I believe I'm still standing in, has been to work toward an understanding of what I am going to do as a result of these reflections. I believe this is where the idea of collaboration surfaces. If I don't want my guilt to turn a blind eye toward international work, then what actions am I going to take? How am I going to ensure that I don't go forward with the mentality "you need these interventions?" How does one safeguard against doing international work for oneself? How do we protect our intentions? I believe it is my guilt that will prevent my intention from turning helping into only feeling good about myself. In order to use my guilt this way I must first take action. That first step is to engage in egalitarian collaboration and to scrutinize the level of equality my relationships exhibit.

I recall being asked to examine further the relationship between client and practitioner as a source of a power differential in my practice and coursework. I've learned that these dimensions require careful self-reflection and conversations. It requires honesty and colleagues with whom you feel comfortable disclosing these self-reflections. I don't believe I could have examined myself more fully without trusting others with my feelings and ideas. I had to share 'Catalina's Guilt' with others. I also attribute this exploration to literature reviews, and not just the U.S. English articles in psychology, but across multiple countries and multiple disciplines. Having guilt doesn't mean that we have to throw out our "U.S.-Articles-In-English-Only-Knowledge", but it also doesn't mean that we can't set it aside. For me, I believe it will be an ongoing challenge, or rather an ongoing *opportunity*. It will require a vigilance to remember not just the more common dimensions of identity that are usually covered, but also the less talked about dimensions of nationality and language. It is a process that I'm still in the midst of experiencing, and to which I thank my guilt for opening.

The Courage to Roll up Our Sleeves: Band-Aids and Bourdain

Daisy Ceja

I am a U.S. born Mexican-American, an English-Spanish bilingual, and a woman. These are some of my identity labels and they influence how I give meaning to things. Global mental health, to me, means the improvement, implementation, and awareness of mental health services available worldwide. Mental health is as important as physical health and the suffering is real whether or not there are signs perceived. Mental health problems are not signs of weakness, and people should be treated with dignity and respect (Lamichhane 2015). Fricchione et al. (2012) suggest that the optimal approach to professional resources in high-income countries and promising health-related institutions in low- and middle-income countries. Being curious about building capacity in global mental health care requires partnerships between the cultural norms of others and inquiring about people's experience, as well as, the interpretation of the experience. This is something I find valuable as a clinician in training. This curiosity is what inspires me to continually turn the kaleidoscope.

My curiosity about global mental health sparked after watching an episode of Anthony Bourdain: No Reservations set in Haiti. Anthony Bourdain is an American chef, author, and television personality that travels the world where he is treated to the local culture and cuisine. In an episode, he visits Haiti after the devastating 2010 earthquake and attempts to dissolve a crowd of hungry people by purchasing all of a vendor's food. This act, feed the hungry, seems reasonable, but inadvertently created mobs of people of all ages and incited violence. The well-intentioned aid effort created a dangerous situation and it demonstrated that interventions might not suffice. Taking the expert stance and applying a band-aid that *we* see as necessary isn't always what individuals need. Is the action, or intervention, towards the vendor in their best interest or in our own? What are the motives behind it? What are the implications?

From my experience, there is a fine line between wanting to help and being helpful. The moral and ethical conflict that may arise between wanting to help and actually being helpful confronts us with the reality that the desire to help is not always sufficient. The moral stance, to me, relates to feeling a duty or responsibility to help as many people as possible. The ethical stance is to restrain your feelings of duty and responsibility if they're going to cause more harm than good. The work I have done with unaccompanied minors crossing the U.S. border has shifted the kaleidoscope and offered me a new perspective. Similar to Anthony Bourdain's experience, I too wanted to jump in, do my part, and do what I set out to do when I joined my Master's program. That is, to provide the best services and make a difference in someone's life. Filled with energy and naiveté, I felt it was my time to make a difference, but I had to remind myself of the moral and ethical stances. Morality and ethics are closely related and the distinction between both is something I continue to juggle and play with.

Through my work with unaccompanied minors, I was reminded that it is easy to actively reject or acknowledge the trauma story of individuals who have endured inhumane situations, what Dr. Mollica (2005) calls the "will to deny." In addition to my initial "will to deny", I was confronted with internal turmoil. This turmoil manifested as a comfort in immediacy, a comfort in swooping in and lending a hand. I reflected back to my moral and ethical stances and began to questions myself. I asked myself "am I doing this to for my client or am I fulfilling a personal need? Am I buying the vendor's fish or am I offering the help the vendor wants?" My concern was intensified when I reflected on Baumgartner and Williams (2014) work that "…teaching people who have experienced and survived oppression and adversity could be considered at best disrespectful and at worst a form of colonization." As a result, it became important for me to be more cognizant of my intentionality, to remember to put aside my expert stance and ask real questions: "What do you want from me?" instead of "what can I give you?"

If I remember the question "what do you want from me?" I can assist and support clients in living out stories that support the growth of their needs and wants instead of my own. Perhaps this could be called a preferred narrative (White 2007). A narrative which could include skills, knowledges, and resources the clients may or may not be already aware of. By remembering this question I believe that the work will be more collaborative, instead of simply swooping in and hastily intervening with a band-aid like Anthony Bourdain.

Reconciling International Differences

Kathryn Dunne

"Are you even married?" I shuddered when she asked me. I can still recall the discomfort and the sharpness of her tone. Have you heard this question before, reader? If I replace it with another adjective does it resonate: straight, Christian, parent, Mexican? Did a client ask you? Did you ask yourself? I have experienced both. I remember the exact day it happened, what I've learned since then is the lasting change this question had on my training. It was a kaleidoscopic shift, albeit a harsh one.

When I began to reflect on my development as an emerging marriage and family therapist I distinctly remember the occasions when my kaleidoscope dramatically turned. While beginning my clinical training at the Community Counseling Service (our university's clinical training site) I recall a specific client ("Nisa") that lent a rough hand in turning my lens. While she came in searching for help, inadvertently she was the one that helped me embrace my curiosities.

Nisa was a Middle Eastern woman from Turkey in her late twenties. I immediately connected with her as I am also a woman in my twenties. I was greatly intrigued and genuinely curious as she arrived elegantly dressed in conservative clothing from head to toe, including the traditional hijab. Nisa had recently immigrated to the United States from Turkey and identified English as her second language. As she began to share her personal narrative with my co-therapist and I (the clinic works from a co-therapy model where two therapists in training provide services at the same time), nervousness due to my unfamiliarity began to arise. She had recently married her husband through an arranged marriage and had only met him once before through video chat. When explaining what had brought her into session that day, she began to explain that she did not love her husband and was not attracted to him sexually. When I inquired further Nisa shared that she had been recently diagnosed with vaginismus and was struggling with the pain she felt during intercourse. The conversation led to her crossroads decision. Nisa did not know if she should remain with her husband because he was nice and respectful, or try to find someone else and divorce him with the certain cultural shame of being an old divorcee.

During the session I tried to stick to one theoretical approach and ask solution focused questions to try and reach a definitive small goal. This is when she expressed her concern for my expertise: "Are you even married?" Nisa explained that she expected someone older with more experience to be helping her, not just a girl in her mid-twenties. Nisa had a specific type of provider in mind. It was an older married woman who knew what it was like to be married, something I could not provide. I could not believe that here was a woman, older by only a couple of years, stating that I did not fit her idea of a marital therapist. This kaleidoscopic shift, although a harsh and uncomfortable one, invited me to position myself more systemically and consider her culture in more detail. At this point in the session I remember turning my own kaleidoscope to Narrative Therapy and began to inquire about her values, cultural upbringing, and her constructions of marriage and therapy. This forceful kaleidoscopic shift furthered my curiosities. It was as if one forceful turn had left it spinning! I began to ask myself questions about my work as a woman. How do I help clients who come from cultural backgrounds that do not consider woman in their mid-twenties to be professionally helpful? Will these clients want to hear what I have to say? Or will they simply discredit me because of my age and gender? These questions propelled me to search further, to read more, and to spin the lens further. What role do I play in this system? How do my lived experiences impact my clients? In my participation in Shoufi Mafi I proceeded to search for these answers. One of these searches led me to what I now consider multiplicity, a variety of lived experiences.

I remember searching for articles to bring to one of our early Shouf Mafi meetings in an effort to continue to find answers. It was a brainstorming session of sorts where we were invited to search for news articles that nurtured our mongoose curiosity. I came across a post online from the social-news website, *Buzzfeed*. It was a summary based an article published by the international news agency *Reuters* which discussed how men in Afghanistan held protests in support of women's rights (Mahr and Harooni 2015). The article went on to state that some of the women were happy to have support, while others felt it disregarded their culture and did not want things to change (Mahr and Harooni 2015). I reflected on this piece after working with Nisa. Simply because she had these specific views of marriage and certain expectations of therapy, did not mean that it was representative of her country. As a woman from the United States in the second year of my master's graduate program in marriage and family therapy, I fell in line with the group of women that welcomed the support; I struggled to understand the women who didn't. I struggled to understand Nisa.

Studying to work as a marriage and family therapist in the mental health field, I am told that my training includes learning to be mindful of the cultures and populations I work with. I am trained to not try to impose my ideas or goals onto clients for the sake of having my idea of a successful session come to fruition. Specifically in my Marriage and Family Therapy coursework I am invited to take the non-expert one down position. It is the clients that are the experts of their own lives. "While we have a knowledge of, or 'expertise' in, the process of therapy, the client is the expert on their own meaning and experience not the therapist" (Moon 2008). Perhaps this idea may not be anything new to you, reader. However, as an emerging marriage and family therapist, I struggle with how I can best serve populations and cultures that are completely foreign to me. By "completely foreign'" I meant that it is something unfamiliar to me, or that perhaps I don't share the culture's values.

When I consider going to international places outside my own country (perhaps even Turkey), am I expected to immerse myself in their cultures and practices so that I can begin to have some understanding of who they are? I began to challenge myself on how can I provide assistance in areas of the world where women may not be allowed to have the education or standing that I already possess and value. As a young woman in my 20s, I'm cognizant that these parts of my identity may place me in a marginalized position in other countries. I also recognize that my U.S. citizenship places me in quite the opposite position. I've realized through my kaleidoscopic shifts that there's a balance, a refocusing of the lens through multiple adjustments. Not just from my own hands but from the multiple hands of others. These adjustments are made within my different contexts and throughout the relationships in my lives, including my clients. In my experience there is nothing more systemic than to reflect on how we are changed by our clients.

Some of these hands that shifted and turned my lens belonged to my fellow Shoufi Mafis. I approached the student working group and tried to tease out these dilemmas; they allowed me to battle with these questions and negotiate the answers. It was a game in multiplicity. With my colleagues, I was able to throw the metaphorical 'question ball' back and forth. Sometimes we were able to catch it and negotiate new answers, sometimes it stayed in the air or landed on the ground to be played with another day. This playfulness allowed us to twist and turn the kaleidoscope, which in turn shifted and challenged us to consider multiplicity.

And Who Is My Neighbor? A Global Effort in Raising Awareness and Promoting Change

Kotia Whitaker

It was 2007. I was a Sergeant in the Army and had been deployed to Bagdad, Iraq. It was the first of many things that year; first time in the Middle-East, first military tour, and the first time I saw a small community of mud huts. While approaching this community during a security operations convoy children began surfacing from their mud huts and running towards the road to meet us. We drove past the children who stood alongside the road, and fellow convoy members began tossing out bottles of water and bags of food. It was a despairing moment for me, as the children looked destitute with their worn-out clothes. Their faces looked aged before their time.

On a very different mission I met community tribal leaders of affluent and prominent status. I immediately noticed the sharp contrast between these two encounters. The tribal leaders were finely dressed, well-groomed, nourished, and lacked the dejected appearance the children possessed. It seemed to me that there was an inequality in the level of impact poverty and conflict has on different individuals. This was a pivotal moment for my lens. My kaleidoscope began to shift as I realized that social context can in fact influence how individuals experience war and conflict. This was only one of the many shifts I attribute to my relationship with the Army.

A second kaleidoscopic shift came at the moment when I began my transition to civilian life. When I was discharged from the military I felt confronted with a new ideology. This ideology differed from the rigid framework I had been trained in. I was straying from themes of uniformity, standard, and order. I was entering the land of fluidity and leaving behind the themes that I related to modernism.

> Within a modernist paradigm it is taken for granted that there is evidence, that there is truth, and that reality or its representation exists to be measured and understood. It is thought that by conducting research we are progressively moving toward an ideal and we will continue to increase our knowledge and understanding of what makes our work more effective, thereby improving the practices and services of all involved (Ramey and Grubb 2009, p. 76).

By losing the paradigm of absolute truths I felt that I was losing what was familiar and comfortable. I remember sitting in my Introduction to Systemic Approaches to Psychotherapy and feeling like I was in the realm of the unfamiliar. I felt intrigued as I was introduced to the fluid framework that is the foundation of my training as a marriage and family therapist. I also felt confronted with the postmodern conclusion that Nietzsche offers, "there are no eternal facts, no absolute truths" (as cited in Meyer 2010, p. 139); a confrontation that battled with my modernist Christian beliefs. With the dissonance between these two opposing paradigms I was challenged to explore my personal beliefs and find a balance that would not conflict with my responsibilities to the client. I turned to a modernist source of truths to reconcile these conflicting paradigms. I turned to my Bible.

"Who is my neighbor?" A man asks in order to judge who he should or shouldn't care for. This is the moment when Jesus offers the Parable of the Good Samaritan. This Samaritan man, who should have been the least likely to help, stopped and rendered aid above what was necessary to a robbed and beaten man lying on a road. At the same time those that were expected to help passed on the opposite side of the road. This parable taught me to refrain from only helping my neighbor but instead to show love and compassion for those who I interact with regardless of my personal truths. I found that practicing the mind of Christ was the solution for maintaining the harmony between Biblical modernism and postmodern therapy (Luke 10:25–37 New International Version).

At the same time the beginning of this shift, or turn of the lens, could not be stopped or backtracked. I was caught between two worlds, what I parallel with the experience of hyphenation (Chinese-Canadian) and living in between the hyphen (Thompson and Nakagawa 2006). This middle ground, or hyphen life of modernist-postmodernist, was a context all its own. It was a mix of my modernist military background and my recent transition to postmodern civilian life. It is no longer extremes of either or for me but a mixture of both. I still find the utility of methodology and structured frameworks in my military service as essential, yet I also recognize that it can be limiting and stagnant. While I thought I was shifting my paradigm from a modernist to postmodernist lens, what I was really doing was living in both (and neither) at the same time. As I began to discern these opposing paradigms I also started to reconcile them, to construct a new meaning. I chose to construct the belief that these paradigm neighbors can live harmoniously. In this harmony I developed my own paradigm.

My paradigm is a construction of family therapy consisting of an exploration of the problem from the family system's perspective. It does not require the client to conform to rigidity or uniformity. I further extend this construction to include a global perspective. I believe that the countries and discourses offer contexts that individuals inhabit. These contexts can be oppressive, marginalizing, and rigid. Families are microcosms of larger systems, they are systems within systems. My experience in the Army has become a first-hand account of this realization. Due to my lived experiences I have begun to understand how pivotal our paradigms and perspectives are on the work that we offer to clients. Furthermore, I believe it is a chosen philosophical stance that influences more than just our 9-5 s, but our daily lives as well.

> These questions are not mere philosophical discussions to be left to the philosophically inclined, or to those who have the time to engage in incessant philosophical banter about the nature of knowledge; rather, they are ethical positions, which are of primary concern to both modernist and postmodernist researchers and practitioners, and which appear to dictate very different attitudes and behaviors when it comes to what constitutes good mental health practice. (Ramey and Grubb 2009, p. 77)

Through my writing I hope that my hyphenated life of modernism-postmodernism will continue to shift and turn my kaleidoscope and those of other practitioners. As a philosophical stance I choose to believe that these discussions are essential. It is in the shifting and the turning of the lens that I find out more about myself, and I invite you to welcome in the uncertainty.

Shifts and Turns: Kaleidoscopic Ends

Catalina Perdomo

A kaleidoscope is an object that is made to be turned. It is eternally changing, never quite the same, and fluid. It is the perfect analogy for our work as marriage and family therapists in training. It was clear to us that it is necessary to make visible the contexts in which we have shaped our personal lives and biases because it affects our practice. The mongoose curiosity and the shifting of the kaleidoscope are ever present, not just as emerging clinicians but also as contextual beings with unique lived experiences. We have found it useful to be eternally open to the shifts and the processing as we adjust, sometimes uncomfortably. Our hope is that Shoufi Mafis will begin to surface elsewhere, for the student group context allowed for self-discoveries. We felt it important, nay dutiful, to share our vulnerabilities, curiosities, and personal struggles in an effort to aid others in their own journeys as students, practitioners, and contextual beings. In true kaleidoscopic fashion, we believe that what we shared here will not remain stagnant, in fact it is already changing as you read. With this fluidity in mind we invite you to embrace your ever shifting lens, for what better way is there to nourish your curiosities?

References

Andersen, T. (1997). Researching client-therapist relationships: A collaborative study for informing therapy. *Journal of Systemic Therapies, 16*(2), 125–133.

Baumgartner, B., & Williams, B. D. (2014). Becoming an insider: Narrative therapy groups alongside people overcoming homelessness. *Journal of Systemic Therapies, 33*(4), 1–14. doi:10.1521/jsyt.2014.33.4.1.

Charlés, L. (2015, July). Long live Shoufi Mafi! Family therapy in the age of global mental health. *Family Therapy Magazine*, 34–39.

Fricchione, G. L., Borba, C. C., Alem, A., Shibre, T., Carney, J. R., & Henderson, D. C. (2012). Capacity building in global mental health: Professional training. *Harvard Review of Psychiatry, 20*(1), 47–57. doi:10.3109/10673229.2012.655211.

Kipling, R. (1894). *The jungle book*. London: Macmillan Publishing.

Lamichhane, J. (2015). Dignity in mental health. Retrieved from http://mhinnovation.net/blog/2015/oct/27/dignity-mental-health.VkVZxYTc7dm.

Mahr, K., & Harooni, M. (2015, March 5). Afghan men don burqas, take to the streets for women's rights. Retrieved from http://www.reuters.com/article/us-afghanistan-women-burqa-idUSKBN0M11BJ20150305.

McIntosh, P. (1988). *White privilege and male privilege: A personal account of coming to see correspondences through work in women's studies*. Wellesley, MA: Wellesley College, Center for Research on Women.

Meyer, M. (2010). *Reading Nietzsche through the ancients*. Boston, MA: Walter de Gruyter Inc.

Mollica, R. (2005). The transfiguration of healing: The care of survivors of mass violence and torture. Retrieved from https://www.youtube.com/watch?v=4_d3wmEslcc.

Moon, L. (Ed.). (2008). *Feeling queer or queer feelings?: Radical approaches to counselling sex, sexualities and genders*. London, England: Routledge.

Platt, J., & Laszloffy, T. (2013). Critical patriotism: Incorporating nationality into MFT education and training. *Journal of Marital and Family Therapy, 39*(4), 441–456. doi:10.1111/j.1752-0606.2012.00325.x.

Ramey, H. L., & Grubb, S. (2009). Modernism, postmodernism and (evidence-based) practice. *Contemporary Family Therapy: An International Journal, 31*(2), 75–86. doi:10.1007/s10591-009-9086-6.

Rothenberg, P. (2002). *White privilege: Essential readings on the other side of racism*. New York, NY: Worth.

Tervalon, M., & Murray-García, J. (1998). Cultural humility versus cultural competence: A critical distinction in defining physician training outcomes in multicultural education. *Journal of Health Care for the Poor and Underserved, 9*(2), 117–125.

Thompson, B. (Producer), & Nakagawa, A.M. (Director). (2006). (2006). *Between: Living in the hyphen [motion picture]*. Princeton, NJ: Films Media Group, Films for the Humanities & Sciences.

White, M. (2007). *MAPS of narrative practice*. New York, NY: W. W. Norton.

Made in the USA
San Bernardino, CA
08 December 2016